Social Media Mining with R

Deploy cutting-edge sentiment analysis techniques
to real-world social media data using R

Nathan Danneman

Richard Heimann

[PACKT] open source*
PUBLISHING   community experience distilled

BIRMINGHAM - MUMBAI

Social Media Mining with R

First published: March 2014

Production Reference: 1180314

Published by Packt Publishing Ltd.
Livery Place
35 Livery Street
Birmingham B3 2PB, UK.

ISBN 978-1-78328-177-0

www.packtpub.com

Cover Image by Monseé G. Wood (monsee.wood@vgrtech.com)

Credits

About the Authors

Nathan Danneman holds a PhD degree from Emory University, where he studied International Conflict. Recently, his technical areas of research have included the analysis of textual and geospatial data and the study of multivariate outlier detection.

Nathan is currently a data scientist at Data Tactics, and supports programs at DARPA and the Department of Homeland Security.

> I would like to thank my father, for pushing me to think analytically, and my mother, who taught me that the most interesting thing to think about is people.

Richard Heimann leads the Data Science Team at Data Tactics Corporation and is an EMC Certified Data Scientist specializing in spatial statistics, data mining, Big Data, and pattern discovery and recognition. Since 2005, Data Tactics has been a premier Big Data and analytics service provider based in Washington D.C., serving customers globally.

Richard is an adjunct faculty member at the University of Maryland, Baltimore County, where he teaches spatial analysis and statistical reasoning. Additionally, he is an instructor at George Mason University, teaching human terrain analysis, and is also a selection committee member for the 2014-2015 AAAS Big Data and Analytics Fellowship Program.

In addition to co-authoring *Social Media Mining in R*, Richard has also recently reviewed *Making Big Data Work for Your Business* for *Packt Publishing,* and also writes frequently on related topics for the Big Data Republic (`http://www.bigdatarepublic.com/bloggers.asp#Rich_Heimann`). He has recently assisted DARPA, DHS, the US Army, and the Pentagon with analytical support.

> I'd like to thank my mother who has been supportive and still makes every effort to understand and contribute to my thinking.

About the Reviewers

Carlos J. Gil Bellosta is a data scientist who originally trained as a mathematician. He has worked as a freelance statistical consultant for 10 years. Among his many projects, he participated in the development of several natural language processing tools for the Spanish language in Molino de Ideas, a startup based in Madrid. He is currently a senior data scientist at eBay in Zurich.

He is an R enthusiast and has developed several R packages, and is also an active member of the R community in his native Spain. He is one of the founders and the first president of the Comunidad R Hispano, the association of R users in Spain. He has also participated in the organization of the yearly conferences on R in Spain.

Finally, he is an active blogger and writes on statistics, data mining, natural language processing, and all things numerical at `http://www.datanalytics.com`.

Vibhav Vivek Kamath holds a master's degree in Industrial Engineering and Operations Research from the Indian Institute of Technology, Bombay and a bachelor's degree in Electronics Engineering from the College of Engineering, Pune. During his post-graduation, he was intrigued by algorithms and mathematical modelling, and has been involved in analytics ever since. He is currently based out of Bangalore, and works for an IT services firm. As part of his job, he has developed statistical/mathematical models based on techniques such as optimization and linear regression using the R programming language. He has also spent quite some time handling data visualization and dashboarding for a leading global bank using platforms such as SAS, SQL, and Excel/VBA.

In the past, he has worked on areas such as discrete event simulation and speech processing (both on MATLAB) as part of his academics. He likes building hobby projects in Python and has been involved in robotics in the past. Apart from programming, Vibhav is interested in reading and likes both fiction and non-fiction. He plays table tennis in his free time, follows cricket and tennis, and likes solving puzzles (Sudoku and Kakuro) when really bored. You can get in touch with him at vibhav.kamath@hotmail.com with regards to any of the topics above or anything else interesting for that matter!

Feng Mai is currently a PhD candidate in the Department of Operations, Business Analytics, and Information Systems at Carl H. Lindner College of Business, University of Cincinnati. He received a BA in Mathematics from Wabash College and an MS in Statistics from Miami University. He has taught undergraduate business core courses such as business statistics and decision models. His research interests include user-generated content, supply chain analytics, and quality management. His work has been published in journals such as *Marketing Science* and *Quality Management Journal*.

Ajay Ohri is the founder of the analytics startup `Decisionstats.com`. He has pursued graduate studies at the University of Tennessee, Knoxville and the Indian Institute of Management, Lucknow. In addition, Ohri has a mechanical engineering degree from the Delhi College of Engineering. He has interviewed more than 100 practitioners in analytics, including leading members from all the analytics software vendors. Ohri has written almost 1,300 articles on his blog, besides guest writing for influential analytics communities. He teaches courses in R through online education and has worked as an analytics consultant in India for the past decade. Ohri was one of the earliest independent analytics consultants in India, and his current research interests include spreading open source analytics and analyzing social media manipulation, simpler interfaces to cloud computing, and unorthodox cryptography. He is the author of *R for Business Analytics*.

Yanchang Zhao is a senior data miner in the Australian public sector. Before joining the public sector, he was an Australian postdoctoral fellow (industry) at the University of Technology, Sydney from 2007 to 2009. He is the founder of the RDataMining website (`http://www.rdatamining.com/`) and RDataMining Group on LinkedIn. He has rich experience in R and data mining. He started his research on data mining in 2001 and has been applying data mining in real-world business applications since 2006. He is a senior member of IEEE, and has been a program chair of the Australasian Data Mining Conference (AusDM) in 2012-2013 and a program committee member for more than 50 academic conferences. He has over 50 publications on data mining research and applications, including two books on R and data mining. The first book is *Data Mining Applications with R*, which features 15 real-world applications on data mining with R, and the second book is *R and Data Mining: Examples and Case Studies*, which introduces readers to using R for data mining with examples and case studies.

www.PacktPub.com

Support files, eBooks, discount offers and more

You might want to visit www.PacktPub.com for support files and downloads related to your book.

Did you know that Packt offers eBook versions of every book published, with PDF and ePub files available? You can upgrade to the eBook version at www.PacktPub.com and as a print book customer, you are entitled to a discount on the eBook copy. Get in touch with us at service@packtpub.com for more details.

At www.PacktPub.com, you can also read a collection of free technical articles, sign up for a range of free newsletters and receive exclusive discounts and offers on Packt books and eBooks.

http://PacktLib.PacktPub.com

Do you need instant solutions to your IT questions? PacktLib is Packt's online digital book library. Here, you can access, read and search across Packt's entire library of books.

Why Subscribe?
- Fully searchable across every book published by Packt
- Copy and paste, print and bookmark content
- On demand and accessible via web browser

Free Access for Packt account holders

If you have an account with Packt at www.PacktPub.com, you can use this to access PacktLib today and view nine entirely free books. Simply use your login credentials for immediate access.

Table of Contents

Preface   1

Chapter 1: Going Viral   7
  Social media mining using sentiment analysis   7
  The state of communication   8
  What is Big Data?   10
  Human sensors and honest signals   12
  Quantitative approaches   15
  Summary   17

Chapter 2: Getting Started with R   19
  Why R?   19
  Quick start   22
    The basics – assignment and arithmetic   23
    Functions, arguments, and help   23
  Vectors, sequences, and combining vectors   25
  A quick example – creating data frames and importing files   26
  Visualization in R   28
  Style and workflow   30
  Additional resources   30
  Summary   31

Chapter 3: Mining Twitter with R   33
  Why Twitter data?   33
  Obtaining Twitter data   34
  Preliminary analyses   38
  Summary   42

Chapter 4: Potentials and Pitfalls of Social Media Data | 43

Opinion mining made difficult | 43
Sentiment and its measurement | 44
The nature of social media data | 46
Traditional versus nontraditional social data | 46
Measurement and inferential challenges | 47
Summary | 51

Chapter 5: Social Media Mining – Fundamentals | 53

Key concepts of social media mining | 53
Good data versus bad data | 54
Understanding sentiments | 56
   Scherer's typology of emotions | 56
Sentiment polarity – data and classification | 57
Supervised social media mining – lexicon-based sentiment | 59
Supervised social media mining – Naive Bayes classifiers | 61
Unsupervised social media mining – Item Response Theory for text scaling | 62
Summary | 64

Chapter 6: Social Media Mining – Case Studies | 65

Introductory considerations | 65
Case study 1 – supervised social media mining – lexicon-based sentiment | 67
Case study 2 – Naive Bayes classifier | 86
Case study 3 – IRT models for unsupervised sentiment scaling | 91
Summary | 98

Appendix: Conclusions and Next Steps | 99

Final thoughts | 99
An expanding field | 100
Further reading | 101
Bibliography | 102

Index | 105

Preface

If you have ever been interested in social media, machine learning, data science, statistical programming, or particularly Big Data—as it relates to extracting value from the data on the Web—then this book is for you. We are excited to provide an introduction to these topics based on our applied research experience. *Social Media Mining with R* exposes readers to both introductory and advanced sentiment analysis techniques through detailed examples and with a large dose of rigorous social science background. Additionally, this book introduces a novel, unsupervised sentiment analysis model. These techniques can be complex, often counterintuitive, and are nearly always laden with assumptions. This book provides readers with a how-to guide for implementing these models and, most importantly, explains the techniques in depth so users can deploy them appropriately and interpret their results correctly. It explains the theoretical grounds for the techniques described and serves to bridge the potential of social media, the theoretical issues surrounding its use, and the practical necessities of its implementation. *Social Media Mining with R* lays out valid arguments for the value of big social media data. The book provides step-by-step instructions on how to obtain, process, and analyze a variety of socially generated data as well as a theoretical background for helping researchers interpret and articulate their findings. The book includes R code and example data that can be used as a springboard as readers undertake their own analyses of business, social, or political data. Readers are not assumed to know R or statistical analysis but are pragmatically provided with the tools required to execute sophisticated data mining techniques on data from the Web.

Overall, *Social Media Mining with R* provides a theoretical background, comprehensive instructions, and state-of-the-art techniques such that readers will be well equipped to embark on their own analyses of social media data.

Thank you for reading!

What this book covers

Chapter 1, Going Viral, introduces the readers to the concept of social media mining, sentiment analysis, the nature of contemporary online communication, and the facets of Big Data that allow social media mining to be such a powerful tool. Additionally, we provide some evidence of the potential and pitfalls of socially generated data and argue for the use of quantitative approaches to social media mining.

Chapter 2, Getting Started with R, highlights the benefits of using R for social media mining. Readers are then walked through the processes of installing, getting help for, and using R. By the end of this chapter, readers would become familiar with data import/export, arithmetic, vectors, basic statistical modeling, and basic graphing using R.

Chapter 3, Mining Twitter with R, explains that an obvious prerequisite to gleaning insight from social media data is obtaining the data itself. Rather than presuming that readers have social media data at their disposal, this chapter demonstrates how to obtain and process such data. It specifically lays out a technical foundation for collecting Twitter data in order to perform social data mining and provides some foundational knowledge and intuition about visualization.

Chapter 4, Potentials and Pitfalls of Social Media Data, highlights that measurement and inference can be challenging when dealing with socially generated data, including social media data. This chapter makes readers aware of common measurement and inference mistakes and demonstrates how these failures can be avoided in applied research settings.

Chapter 5, Social Media Mining – Fundamentals, aims to develop theory and intuition over the models presented in the final chapter. These theoretical insights are provided prior to the step-by-step model building instructions so that researchers can be aware of the assumptions that underpin each model, and thus apply them appropriately.

Chapter 6, Social Media Mining – Case Studies, helps to bring everything together in an accessible and tangible concluding chapter. This chapter demonstrates canonical lexicon-based, and supervised sentiment analysis techniques as well as laying out and executing a novel unsupervised sentiment analysis model. Each class of model is worked through in detail, including code, instructions, and best practices. This chapter rests heavily on the theoretical and social science information provided earlier in the book, but can be accessed right away by readers who already have the requisite understanding.

Appendix, Conclusions and Next Steps, wraps everything up with our final thoughts, the scope of the data mining field, and recommendations for further reading.

What you need for this book

Readers will require the open source statistical programming language R (Version 3.0 or higher) and are encouraged to use their favorite development environment. R is available at `http://www.r-project.org`. We prefer to use RStudio as our environment, which is available at `http://www.rstudio.com/ide/download/`.

Who this book is for

This book is appropriate for a wide audience. The thorough and careful introduction to social media, sentiment analysis, measurement, and inference make it appropriate for people with technical skills but little social science background. The introduction to R makes the book appropriate for people who lack any sort of programming background. The inclusion of well-studied, canonical sentiment analysis methods makes the book ideal for an introduction to this area of research, while the development of an entirely novel, unsupervised sentiment analysis model will be of interest to the advanced research community.

Conventions

In this book, you will find a number of styles of text that distinguish between different kinds of information. Here are some examples of these styles, and an explanation of their meaning.

R code is shown in the standard manner, where pound signs (#) are used to comment out code or to add unexecuted notes that add intuition about the code. The greater than sign (>) is used to show a new line of executed code. Readers can often expect some output to be added following the greater than sign to show the output from the execution.

Code words in text, database table names, folder names, filenames, file extensions, pathnames, dummy URLs, user input, and Twitter handles are shown as follows: "Though there are several packages that do this, we prefer the `twitteR` package for its ease of use and flexibility."

A block of code is set as follows:

```
> install.packages("twitteR")
> library(twitteR)
```

New terms and important words are shown in bold. Words that you see on the screen, in menus or dialog boxes for example, appear in the text like this: "Now, simply click on the **Create New Application** button and enter the requested information."

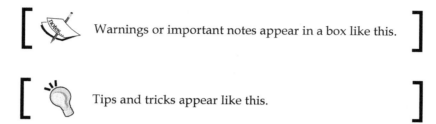

Warnings or important notes appear in a box like this.

Tips and tricks appear like this.

Reader feedback

Feedback from our readers is always welcome. Let us know what you think about this book—what you liked or may have disliked. Reader feedback is important for us to develop titles that you really get the most out of.

To send us general feedback, simply send an e-mail to feedback@packtpub.com, and mention the book title via the subject of your message.

Alternately, you can contact the authors via their Twitter page: Richard Heimann @rheimann and Nathan Danneman @NDanneman.

If there is a topic that you have expertise in and you are interested in either writing or contributing to a book, see our author guide on www.packtpub.com/authors.

Customer support

Now that you are the proud owner of a Packt book, we have a number of things to help you to get the most from your purchase.

Downloading the example code

You can download the example code files for all Packt books you have purchased from your account at http://www.packtpub.com. If you purchased this book elsewhere, you can visit http://www.packtpub.com/support and register to have the files e-mailed directly to you.

Downloading the color images of this book

We also provide you a PDF file that has color images of the screenshots/diagrams used in this book. The color images will help you better understand the changes in the output. You can download this file from: http://www.packtpub.com/sites/default/files/downloads/1770OS_Images.pdf

Errata

Although we have taken every care to ensure the accuracy of our content, mistakes do happen. If you find a mistake in one of our books—maybe a mistake in the text or the code—we would be grateful if you would report this to us. By doing so, you can save other readers from frustration and help us improve subsequent versions of this book. If you find any errata, please report them by visiting http://www.packtpub.com/submit-errata, selecting your book, clicking on the errata submission form link, and entering the details of your errata. Once your errata are verified, your submission will be accepted and the errata will be uploaded on our website, or added to any list of existing errata, under the Errata section of that title. Any existing errata can be viewed by selecting your title from http://www.packtpub.com/support.

Piracy

Piracy of copyright material on the Internet is an ongoing problem across all media. At Packt, we take the protection of our copyright and licenses very seriously. If you come across any illegal copies of our works, in any form, on the Internet, please provide us with the location address or website name immediately so that we can pursue a remedy.

Please contact us at copyright@packtpub.com with a link to the suspected pirated material.

We appreciate your help in protecting our authors, and our ability to bring you valuable content.

Questions

You can contact us at questions@packtpub.com if you are having a problem with any aspect of the book, and we will do our best to address it.

1
Going Viral

In this chapter, we introduce readers to the concept of social media mining. We discuss sentiment analysis, the nature of contemporary online communication, and the facets of Big Data that allow social media mining to be such a powerful tool. Additionally, we discuss some of the potential pitfalls of socially generated data and argue for a quantitative approach to social media mining.

Social media mining using sentiment analysis

People are highly opinionated. We hold opinions about everything from international politics to pizza delivery. Sentiment analysis, synonymously referred to as opinion mining, is the field of study that analyzes people's opinions, sentiments, evaluations, attitudes, and emotions through written language. Practically speaking, this field allows us to measure, and thus harness, opinions. Up until the last 40 years or so, opinion mining hardly existed. This is because opinions were elicited in surveys rather than in text documents, computers were not powerful enough to store or sort a large amount of information, and algorithms did not exist to extract opinion information from written language.

The explosion of sentiment-laden content on the Internet, the increase in computing power, and advances in data mining techniques have turned social data mining into a thriving academic field and crucial commercial domain. Professor Richard Hamming famously pushes researchers to ask themselves, "What are the important problems in my field?" Researchers in the broad area of **natural language processing** (**NLP**) cannot help but list sentiment analysis as one such pressing problem. Sentiment analysis is not only a prominent and challenging research area, but also a powerful tool currently being employed in almost every business and social domain. This prominence is due, at least in part, to the centrality of opinions as both measures and causes of human behavior.

This book is an introduction to social data mining. For us, social data refers to data generated by people or by their interactions. More specifically, social data for the purposes of this book will usually refer to data in text form produced by people for other people's consumption. Data mining is a set of tools and techniques used to describe and make inferences about data. We approach social data mining with a potent mix of applied statistics and social science theory. As for tools, we utilize and provide an introduction to the statistical programming language R.

The book covers important topics and latest developments in the field of social data mining with many references and resources for continued learning. We hope it will be of interest to an audience with a wide array of substantive interests from fields such as marketing, sociology, politics, and sales. We have striven to make it accessible enough to be useful for beginners while simultaneously directing researchers and practitioners already active in the field towards resources for further learning. Code and additional material will be available online at `http://socialmediaminingr.com` as well as on the authors' GitHub account, `https://github.com/SocialMediaMininginR`.

The state of communication

The state of communication section describes the fundamentally altered modes of social communication fostered by the Internet. The interconnected, social, rapid, and public exchange of information detailed here underlies the power of social data mining. Now more than ever before, information can **go viral**, a phrase first cited as early as 2004.

By changing the manner in which we connect with each other, the Internet changed the way we interact—communication is now bi-directional and many-to-many. Networks are now self-organized, and information travels along every dimension, varying systematically depending on direction and purpose. This new economy with ideas as currency has impacted nearly every person. More than ever, people rely on context and information before making decisions or purchases, and by extension, more and more on peer effects and interactions rather than centralized sources.

The traditional modes of communication are represented mainly by radio and television, which are isotropic and one-to-many. It took 38 years for radio broadcasters and 13 years for television to reach an audience of 50 million, but the Internet did it in just four years (Gallup).

Not only has the nature of communication changed, but also its scale. There were 50 pages on the **World Wide Web (WWW)** in 1993. Today, the full impact and scope of the WWW is difficult to measure, but we can get a rough sense of its size: the Indexed Web contains at least 1.7 billion pages as of February 2014 (World Wide Web size). The WWW is the largest, most widely used source of information, with nearly 2.4 billion users (Wikipedia). 70 percent of these users use it daily to both contribute and receive information in order to learn about the world around them and to influence that same world—constantly organizing information around pieces that reflect their desires.

In today's connected world, many of us are members of at least one, if not more, social networking service. The influence and reach of social media enterprises such as Facebook is staggering. Facebook has 1.11 billion monthly active users and 751 million monthly active users of their mobile products (Facebook key facts). Twitter has more than 200 million (Twitter blog) active users. As communication tools, they offer a global reach to huge multinational audiences, delivering messages almost instantaneously.

Connectedness and social media have altered the way we organize our communications. Today we have dramatically more friends and more friends of friends, and we can communicate with these higher order connections faster and more frequently than ever before. It is difficult to ignore the abundance of mimicry (that is, copying or reposting) and repeated social interactions in our social networks. This mimicry is a result of virtual social interactions organized into reaffirming or oppositional feedback loops. We self-organize these interactions via (often preferential) attachments that form organic, shifting networks. There is little question of whether or not social media has already impacted your life and changed the manner in which you communicate. Our beliefs and perceptions of reality, as well as the choices we make, are largely conditioned by our neighbors in virtual and physical networks. When we need to make a decision, we seek out for opinions of others—more and more of those opinions are provided by virtual networks.

Information bounce is the resonance of content within and between social networks often powered by social media such as customer reviews, forums, blogs, microblogs, and other user-generated content. This notion represents a significant change when compared to how information has traveled throughout history; individuals no longer need to exclusively rely on close ties within their physical social networks. Social media has both made our close ties closer and the number of weak ties exponentially greater. Beyond our denser and larger social networks is a general eagerness to incorporate information from other networks with similar interests and desires. The increased access to networks of various types has, in fact, conditioned us to seek even more information; after all, ignoring available information would constitute irrational behavior.

These fundamental changes to the nature and scope of communication are crucial due to the importance of ideas in today's economic and social interactions. Today, and in the future, ideas will be of central importance, especially those ideas that bounce and go viral. Ideas that go viral are those that resonate and spur on social movements, which may have political and social purposes or reshape businesses and allow companies such as Nike and Apple to produce outsized returns on capital. This book introduces readers to the tools necessary to measure ideas and opinions derived from social data at scale. Along the way, we'll describe strategies for dealing with Big Data.

What is Big Data?

People create 2.5 quintillion bytes (2.5 * 1018) of data, or nearly 2.3 million Terabytes of data every day, so much that 90 percent of the data in the world today has been created in the last two years alone. Furthermore, rather than being a large collection of disparate data, much of this data flow consists of data on similar things, generating huge data-sets with billions upon billions of observations. Big Data refers not only to the deluge of data being generated, but also to the astronomical size of data-sets themselves. Both factors create challenges and opportunities for data scientists.

This data comes from everywhere: physical sensors used to gather information, human sensors such as the social web, transaction records, and cell phone GPS signals to name a few. This data is not only big but is growing at an increasing rate. The data used in this book, namely, Twitter data, is no exception. Twitter was launched in March 21, 2006, and it took 3 years, 2 months, and 1 day to reach 1 billion tweets. Twitter users now send 1 billion tweets every 2.5 days.

What proportion of data is Big Data? It turns out that most data-sets are (relatively) small. This may come as a surprise in light of the contemporary excitement surrounding Big Data. The reason for the large number of small data-sets is that data that is not socially generated and publicly displayed is time consuming and expensive to collect. As such, academics, businesses, and other organizations with data needs tend to collect only the minimum amount of information necessary to gain purchase on their questions. These data-sets are usually small and focused and are curated by the organizations that use them; they usually do not plan on updating or adding fresh data to them. The poor management of these data often leads to their misplacement, thereby generating dark data—data that is suspected to exist or ought to exist but is difficult or impossible to find. The problem of dark data is real and prevalent in the myriad of small, locally collected data-sets. The utter lack of central management of data in the tail of the data size distribution invariably causes these sets of data to be forgotten. In spite of the fact that most data is not big, it is primarily the Big Data sets that exhibit exponential growth, propelling the number of bytes created by humans moving upwards daily.

Big Data differs substantially from other data not only in its size and velocity, but also in its scope and density. Big Data is large in scope, that is, it is created by everyone and by itself and thus is informative about a wide audience. This characteristic makes it very useful for studying populations, as the inferences we can make generalize to large groups of people. Compare that with, say, opinions gleaned from a focus group or small survey. These opinions, while highly accurate and easy to obtain, may or may not be reflective of the views of the wider public. Thus, Big Data's scope is a real benefit, at least in terms of generalizing evidence to wide populations.

However, Big Data's density is fairly low. By density, we mean the degree to which Big Data, and especially social data, is directly applicable to questions we want to answer. Again, a comparison to small data is useful. Prior to the explosion of Big Data and the proliferation of tools used to harness it, companies or political campaigns largely used focus groups or surveys to obtain information about public sentiments relevant to their endeavors. The focus groups and surveys furnished organizations with data that was directly applicable to their purpose, and often this data would already be measured with meaningful units. For instance, respondents would describe how much they liked or disliked a new product, or rate a political candidate's TV appearances from 1 to 5. Compare that with social data, where opinion-laden text is buried among terabytes of unrelated information and comes in a form that must be subjected to analysis just to generate a measure of the opinion. Thus, low density of big social data presents unique challenges to organizations trying to utilize opinion data.

The size and scope of Big Data helps us overcome some of the hurdles caused by its low density. For instance, even though each unique piece of social data may have little applicability to our particular task, these small bits of information quickly become useful as we aggregate them across thousands or millions of people. Like the proverbial bundle of sticks — none of which could support inferences alone — when tied together, these small bits of information can be a powerful tool for understanding the opinions of the online populace.

The sheer scope of Big Data has other benefits as well. The size and coverage of many social data-sets creates coverage overlaps in time, space, and topic. This allows analysts to cross-refer socially generated sets against one another or against small-scale data-sets designed to examine niche questions. This type of cross-coverage can generate consilience (Osborne) — the principle that states evidence from independent, unrelated sources can converge to form strong conclusions. That is, when multiple sources of evidence are in agreement, the conclusion can be very strong even when none of the individual sources of evidence are very strong on their own. A crucial characteristic of socially generated data is that it is opinionated. This point underpins the usefulness of big social data for sentiment analysis, and is novel. For the first time in history, interested parties can put their fingers to the pulse of the masses because the masses are frequently opining about what is important to them. They opine with and for each other and anyone else who cares to listen. In sum, opinionated data is the great enabler of opinion-based research.

Human sensors and honest signals

Opinion data generated by humans in real time presents tremendous opportunities. However, big social data will only prove useful to the extent that it is valid. This section tackles the extent to which socially generated data can be used to accurately measure individual and/or group-level opinions head-on.

One potential indicator of the validity of socially generated data is the extent of its consumption for factual content. Online media has expanded significantly over the past 20 years. For example, online news is displacing print and broadcast. More and more Americans distrust mainstream media, with a majority (60 percent) now having little to no faith in traditional media to report news fully, accurately, and fairly. Instead, people are increasingly turning to the Internet to research, connect, and share opinions and views. This was especially evident during the 2012 election where social media played a large role in information transmission (Gallup).

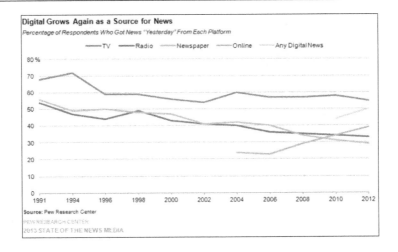

Politics is not the only realm affected by social Big Data. People are increasingly relying on the opinions of others to inform about their consumption preferences. Let's have a look at this:

- 91 percent of people report having gone into a store because of an online experience
- 89 percent of consumers conduct research using search engines
- 62 percent of consumers end up making a purchase in a store after researching it online
- 72 percent of consumers trust online reviews as much as personal recommendations
- 78 percent of consumers say that posts made by companies on social media influence their purchases

If individuals are willing to use social data as a touchstone for decision making in their own lives, perhaps this is prima facie evidence of its validity. Other Big Data thinkers point out that much of what people do online constitutes their genuine actions and intentions. The breadcrumbs left from when people execute online transactions, send messages, or spend time on web pages constitute what *Alex Petland* of MIT calls honest signals. These signals are honest insofar as they are actions taken by people with no subtext or secondary intent. Specifically, he writes the following:

> *"Those breadcrumbs tell the story of your life. It tells what you've chosen to do. That's very different than what you put on Facebook. What you put on Facebook is what you would like to tell people, edited according to the standards of the day. Who you actually are is determined by where you spend time, and which things you buy."*

To paraphrase, *Petland* finds some web-based data to be valid measures of people's attitudes when that data is without subtext or secondary intent; what he calls data exhaust. In other words, actions are harder to fake than words. He cautions against taking people's online statements at face value, because they may be nothing more than cheap talk.

Anthony Stefanidis of George Mason University also advocates for the use of social data mining. He favorably speaks about its reliability, noting that its size inherently creates a preponderance of evidence. This book takes neither the strong position of *Pentland* and honest signals nor *Stefanidis* and preponderance of evidence. Instead, we advocate a blended approach of curiosity and creativity as well as some healthy skepticism.

Generally, we follow the attitude of *Charles Handy* (*The Empty Raincoat*, 1994), who described the steps to measurement during the Vietnam War as follows:

> *"The first step is to measure whatever can be easily measured. This is OK as far as it goes. The second step is to disregard that which can't be easily measured or to give it an arbitrary quantitative value. This is artificial and misleading. The third step is to presume that what can't be measured easily really isn't important. This is blindness. The fourth step is to say that what can't be easily measured really doesn't exist. This is suicide."*

The social web may not consist of perfect data, but its value is tremendous if used properly and analyzed with care. 40 years ago, a social science study containing millions of observations was unheard of due to the time and cost associated with collecting that much information. The most successful efforts in social data mining will be by those who "measure (all) what is measurable, and make measurable (all) what is not so" (*Rasinkinski*, 2008).

Ultimately, we feel that the size and scope of big social data, the fact that some of it is comprised of honest signals, and the fact that some of it can be validated with other data, lends it validity. In another sense, the "proof is in the pudding". Businesses, governments, and organizations are already using social media mining to good effect; thus, the data being mined must be at least moderately useful.

Another defining characteristic of big social data is the speed with which it is generated, especially when considered against traditional media channels. Social media platforms such as Twitter, but also the web generally, spread news in near-instant bursts. From the perspective of social media mining, this speed may be a blessing or a curse. On the one hand, analysts can keep up with the very fast-moving trends and patterns, if necessary. On the other hand, fast-moving information is subject to mistakes or even abuse.

Following the tragic bombings in Boston, Massachusetts (April 15, 2013), Twitter was instrumental in citizen reporting and provided insight into the events as they unfolded. Law enforcement asked for and received help from general public, facilitated by social media. For example, *Reddit* saw an overall peak in traffic when reports came in that the second suspect was captured. Google Analytics reports that there were about 272,000 users on the site with 85,000 in the news update thread alone. This was the only time in *Reddit's* history other than *Obama AMA* that a thread beat the front page in the ratings (*Reddit*).

The downside of this fast-paced, highly visible public search is that masses can be incorrect. This is exactly what happened; users began to look at the details and photos posted and pieced together their own investigation—as it turned out, the information was incorrect. This was a charged event and created an atmosphere that ultimately undermined the good intentions of many. Other efforts such as those by governments (Wikipedia) and companies (Forbes) to post messages favorable to their position is less than well intentioned. Overall, we should be skeptical of tactical (that is, very real time) uses of social media. However, as evidence and information are aggregated by social media, we expect certain types of data, especially opinions and sentiments, to converge towards the truth (subject to the caveats set out in *Chapter 4, Potentials and Pitfalls of Social Media Data*).

Quantitative approaches

In this research, we aim to mine and summarize online opinions in reviews, tweets, blogs, forum discussions, and so on. Our approach is highly quantitative (that is, mathematical and/or statistical) as opposed to qualitative (that is, involving close study of a few instances). In social sciences, these two approaches are sometimes at odds, or at least their practitioners are. In this section, we will lay out the rationale for a quantitative approach to understanding online opinions. Our use of quantitative approaches is entirely pragmatic rather than dogmatic. We do, however, find the famous *Bill James'* words relating to the quantitative and qualitative tension to resonate with our pragmatic voice.

> *"The alternative to good statistics is not "no statistics", it's bad statistics. People who argue against statistical reasoning often end up backing up their arguments with whatever numbers they have at their command, over- or under-adjusting in their eagerness to avoid anything systematic."*

One traditional rationale for using qualitative approaches to sentiment analysis, such as focus groups, is lack of available data. Looking closely at what a handful of consumers think about a product is a viable way to generate opinion data if none, or very little, exists. However, in the era of big social data, analysts are awash in opinion-laden text and online actions. In fact, the use of statistical approaches is often necessary to handle the sheer volume of data generated by the social web. Furthermore, the explosion of data is obviating traditional hypothesis-testing concerns about sampling, as samples converge in size towards the population of interest.

The exploration of large sets of opinion data is what *Openshaw* (1988) would call a data-rich but theory-poor environment. Often, qualitative methods are well suited for inductively deriving theories from small numbers of test cases. However, our aim as sentiment analyzers is usually less theoretical and more descriptive; that is, we want to measure opinions and not understand the process by which they are generated. As such, this book covers important quantitative methods that reflect the state of discipline and that allow data to have a voice. This type of analysis accomplishes what *Gould* (1981) refers to as "letting the data speak for itself."

Perhaps the strongest reason to choose quantitative methods over qualitative ones is the ability of quantitative methods, when coupled with large and valid data-sets, to generate accurate measures in the face of analyst biases. Qualitative methods, even when applied correctly, put researchers at risk of a plethora of inferential problems. Foremost is apophenia, the human tendency to discover patterns where there are none; for example, a Type I error of sorts and dubbed patternicity by *Michael Shermer* (2008). A second pitfall of qualitative work is the atomistic fallacy, that is, the problem of generalizing based on an insufficient number of individual observations. The atomistic fallacy is real. Most people rely on advice from only a few sources, over-weighting information from within their networks rather than third parties such as Consumers Reports. Allowing an individual observation (for example, an opinion) to influence our actions or decisions is unreliably compared to what constitutes sensible samples in Consumers Reports.

The natural sciences benefited from the invention and proliferation of a host of new measurement tools during the twentieth century. For example, advances in microscopes led to a range of discoveries. The advent of the social web, with its seemingly endless amounts of opinionated data, and new measurement tools such as the ones covered in this book calls for a set of new discoveries. This book introduces readers to tools that will assist in that pursuit.

Summary

In this chapter, we introduced readers to the concepts of social media, sentiment analysis, and Big Data. We described how social media has changed the nature of interpersonal communication and the opportunities it presents for analysts of social data. This chapter also made a case for the use of quantitative approaches to measure all that is measurable, and make the one which is not so measurable.

In the next chapter, we will introduce R, which is the main tool through which we will illustrate techniques for harvesting, analyzing, and visualizing social media data.

2
Getting Started with R

In this chapter, we lay out the case for using R for social media mining. We then walk readers through the processes of installing, getting help for, and using R. By the end of this chapter, readers will have gained familiarity with data import/export, arithmetic, vectors, basic statistical modeling, and basic graphing using R.

Why R?

We strongly prefer using the R statistical computing environment for social data mining. This chapter highlights the benefits of using R, presents an introductory lesson on its use, and provides pointers towards further resources for learning the R language.

At its most basic, R is simply a calculator. You can ask it what 2 + 2 is, and it will provide you with 4 as the answer. However, R is more flexible than the calculator you used in high school. In fact, its flexibility leads it to be described as a statistical computing environment. As such, it comes with functions that assist us with data manipulation, statistics, and graphing. R can also store, handle, and perform complex mathematical operations on data as well as utilize a suite of statistics-specific functions, such as drawing samples from common probability distributions. Most simply, R is data analysis software adoringly promoted as being made by statisticians for statisticians. The R programming language is used by data scientists, statisticians, formal scientists, physical scientists, social scientists, and others who need to make sense of data for statistical analysis, data visualization, and predictive modeling. Fortunately, with the brief guidance provided by this chapter, you too will be using R for your own research. R is simple to learn, even for people with no programming or statistics experience.

R is a **GNU (GNU's Not Unix)** project, where GNU's Not Unix is a recursive acronym for GNU and is less commonly referred to as GNU S. R is freely available under the GNU General Public License, and precompiled binary versions are provided for most common operating systems. R uses a command-line interface; however, several integrated development environments are available for use with R, including our preferred one, RStudio.

The following nine important questions ought to drive whether to use R or some other statistical language:

- Does the software run natively on your computer?
  - R compiles and runs on a variety of Unix platforms as well as on Windows and Mac OS.

- Does the software provide the methods needed?
  - R comes with a moderate compliment of built-in functions and is wildly extensible through user-generated packages from a variety of disciplines.

- If not, how extensible is the software, if at all?
  - R is extremely extensible and extending it is simple. Packages are provided by a robust academic and practitioner community and are available for inclusion through simple downloads.

- Does the software fully support programming versus point-and-click?
  - Users can utilize R as an interactive programming language or a scripting language. There are also packages, such as Rcmdr, that allow limited point-and-click functionality.

- Are the visualization options adequate for your needs?
  - R has a very powerful, simple-to-use suite of graphical capabilities. Additionally, these capabilities are extensible just like R's other capabilities.

- Does the software provide output in the form you prefer?
  - R can output data files in many formats and can produce graphics in a wide range of formats as well.

- Does the software handle large datasets?
  - R handles data in memory; thus, users are constrained by the memory of their local system. However, within that constraint, R can handle vectors of up to 2 gigabytes in length. Packages can extend R to work in cloud computing environments.

- Can you afford the software?
  - R is free, as in free beer.

R is an open source software, which means that members of the public invented it and they now maintain and distribute it, as opposed to a corporation or other private entity. Mainstream reasons to use open source software have historically hinged on the free aspect, that is, free as in free beer. In the past, open source projects have often been plagued with serious drawbacks such as having limited functionality, being buggy, not staying up-to-date, and being difficult to get help with. However, open source projects such as R attract a large community of developers and users to overcome these issues. Furthermore, R has an expansive (and expanding) functionality and is constantly updated; thanks to the large number of people using and developing it, help is nearly always just a Google away. The open source nature of R makes it free, as in free beer, and also free, as in freedom from vendor lock-in, which is what Richard Stallman advocates as the best reason for moving to open source projects. As Mozilla's Firefox browser has commandingly demonstrated, open source software can be excellent and approachable as opposed to being aimed at niche users.

The excellence of R has several consequences, each of which in turn cause R to become better. First and foremost, R is extensible. Individuals can contribute add-on components called packages to R, which execute algorithms, create graphics, or perform other tasks. The number of these packages has grown exponentially over time; as of early 2014, there were over 5,000. Furthermore, many of these packages are multiplicatively useful when combined, making them more valuable as a whole than the sum of their individual utilities.

Secondly, R has a large and growing community of users and contributors, largely due to its excellence and broad utility. R has proven useful to so many that the traffic flow about it on e-mail discussion forums now outstrips the traffic on all of its main commercial contemporaries such as Stata, SAS, and SPSS. Similarly, the traffic related to R on Stack Overflow (http://stackoverflow.com), a software help forum, has outstripped SAS as well as some generic computing languages, such as PERL. Perhaps what's most telling is the fact that, at the time of writing this book (early 2014), more than half of the users on Kaggle (http://www.r-bloggers.com/how-kaggle-competitors-use-r/)—a site that promotes high-end data analysis competitions—use R.

R's popularity is indicative of its quality and broad utility. Additionally, the large number of active users make it much easier to get help with R through forums such as Stack Overflow and others (if R's built-in help documentation doesn't already answer your questions). Additionally, there are many books currently available in print that walk users through how to perform intermediate and advanced general programming in R as well as demonstrate R's use for particular domains (such as this one).

The justification for using R is overwhelming. We find R to have an excellent combination of freedom (both kinds), flexibility, and power. In addition, R has growing capabilities in handling Big Data in distributed systems or in parallel; some examples include **Distributed Storage and List (dsl)**, **HadoopInteractiVE (hive)**, **Text Mining Distributed Corpus Plug-In (tm.plug.dc)**, **Hadoop Steaming (HadoopSteaming)**, and **Amazon Web Services (AWS.tools)**. So, let's get started.

Quick start

To install R, simply navigate to `http://www.r-project.org` and choose a mirror near you. Then, select whether you want R for Linux, Windows, or Mac. Finally, just follow the instructions from there, and you'll be up in no time. For additional FAQs, refer to `http://cran.r-project.org/faqs.html`.

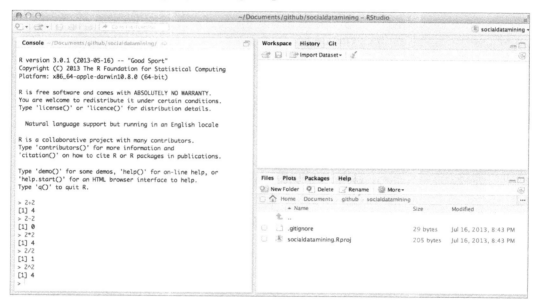

In addition to installing R, you will almost certainly want to install an **integrated development environment** (IDE). An IDE is a programming environment that offers features beyond what is found by using the terminal or a command-line environment. These features can include code editing/highlighting/completion/generation, code compiling, code debugging, a file manager, a package manager, and a **graphical user interface** (GUI). These features will make generating and managing your R code simpler. There are a plethora of options, but we have a slight preference for RStudio, which is shown in the previous screenshot. It is recommended that you install RStudio (`http://www.rstudio.com`) before working through the examples discussed in this book. As we move forward, note that all of the following R code will be available online on the authors' web page and GitHub.

The basics – assignment and arithmetic

R allows access to the central math operators through their standard character representations: exponentiation (^), multiplication (*), division (/), addition (+), and subtraction (-). As you will see in the next example, R respects the order of operations.

The carrot (>) symbol denotes lines of code being inputted to R, while lines without (>) denote the output from R. In some circumstances, R will number its output; we'll point that out as it arises. Finally, R does not read code following a pound sign (#), which allows users to write comments for themselves and others right in the code itself:

```
> 2^4-3
13
> 2^(4-3)
2
```

Downloading the example code

You can download the example code files for all Packt books you have purchased from your account at http://www.packtpub.com. If you purchased this book elsewhere, you can visit http://www.packtpub.com/support and register to have the files e-mailed directly to you.

Functions, arguments, and help

R has many built-in functions. A function is a programming construct that takes input, calls arguments, and turns them into output. Some functions only take one argument. An example of this is as follows:

```
> sqrt(16)
4
```

Other functions take several arguments. Generally, R can use the order in which you provide the arguments to understand the arguments respectively; however, it is a good practice to explicitly label your arguments, which are generally separated by commas. R does not read or care about spaces, but it is a good practice to include spaces between operators and after commas for better readability, as follows:

```
# Take the log of 100 with base 10
> log(100, 10)
2
```

```
# Though not necessary, it is best practice to label arguments
# This avoids confusion when functions take many arguments
> log(100, base=10)
2
```

To get help with a function, you can use the help function or type a question mark before a term. Using double question marks broadens the search, as shown in the following code:

```
> help(log)
> ?log
> ??log
```

Assignment is an important concept in R. We can assign values to an object, then treat that object as if it were the value it stores. An example should make this much more clear. Note the use of the left-facing arrow (<-) for assignment. Although you can assign with a right arrow or a single equals sign, only using the left arrow helps avoid confusion. An example of the assignment concept is shown as follows:

```
# Assign the value 3 to the object called 'my.variable'
> my.variable<- 3
# Work with the object
> my.variable * 2
[1] 6
# Create a new variable
> other.object<- my.variable + 7
> other.object * 2
[1] 20
```

R utilizes logical operators in addition to arithmetic operators. Logical operators are those that compare entities and return values of either TRUE or FALSE. Note that the double equals sign is used to ask a question, while the single equals sign is used for assignment (though the arrow should be strongly preferred for assignment to avoid confusion):

```
> 2==3
[1] FALSE
> 4 >= 4
[1] TRUE
"hello" != "HELLO"
[1] TRUE
```

Vectors, sequences, and combining vectors

Many R operations can be performed, or performed more efficiently, on vectors or matrices. Vectors are strings of objects; matrices are two-dimensional collections of objects, usually numbers. The c operator, which means concatenate, creates simple vectors, while the colon (:) operator generates simple sequences. To construct matrices, one simply passes a vector of data, the dimensions of the matrix to be created, and whether to input the data by row or by column (the default behavior is to input data by row). Examples of vectors, sequences, and matrices are given as follows:

```
> c(1,2,3,4,5)
1 2 3 4 5

> 1:4
1 2 3 4

> 5:-1
5 4 3 2 1 0 -1

> matrix(data=c(1, 2, 3, 4), byrow=TRUE, nrow=2)
1 2
3 4
```

For more complex sequence-like vectors, you can use the seq() function. At a minimum, it takes two arguments: from and to. You can additionally specify a by argument as well:

```
> seq(from=1, to=5)
1 2 3 4 5

> seq(from=2, to=6, by=2)
2 4 6
```

R also contains several constructs that allow access to individual elements or subsets through indexing operations. In the case of basic vector types, one can access the *i* th element by using x[i], but there is also indexing of lists (which are simply collections of other data types), matrices, and multidimensional arrays (that is, matrices with more than two dimensions). In addition, R has a data type called a data frame, which is what many readers familiar with Stata, SPSS, or Microsoft Excel would think of as a dataset or spreadsheet. Data frames have column and possibly row names as well. R has three basic indexing operators, which is displayed in the following examples:

```
x[i]     # read the i-th element of a vector
x[i, j] # read i-th row, j-th column element of a matrix
x[[i]]   # read the i-th element of a list
x$a      # read the variable named "a" in a data frame named x
```

For lists, one generally uses [[to select any single element, whereas [returns a list of the selected elements. Many operators can work over vectors, as shown in the following code:

```
# divides each number in vector by 2
> c(1,2,3,4,5) / 2
0.5 1.0 1.5 2.0 2.5

# first vector divided by second
> c(1,2,3,4,5) / c(5,4,3,2,1)
0.2 0.5 1.0 2.0 5.0

# log base 10 of vector
> log(c(1,2.5,5), base=10)
0.00000 0.39794 0.69897

# new variable x is assigned resultant set
> x <- c(1,2,3,4,5) / 2
> x
0.5 1.0 1.5 2.0 2.5

# generic function 'summary' on variable x
> summary(x)
   Min. 1st Qu.  Median   Mean 3rd Qu.   Max.
    0.5     1.0     1.5    1.5     2.0    2.5

# function to find mean
# notice mean is also captured by the generic function 'summary'
> mean(x)
1.5
```

A quick example – creating data frames and importing files

Getting data into R is often the first step in an analysis. R has a suite of functions called read, such as read.csv(), to help import data. Here, we assign the values read from a CSV file to an object called mydata as shown in the following code:

```
> mydata<- read.csv("http://www.ats.ucla.edu/stat/data/binary.csv")

# returns the first few rows of the data
> head(mydata)
```

```
  admit  gre  gpa rank
1     0 380 3.61    3
2     1 660 3.67    3
3     1 800 4.00    1
```

To the initial confusion of some, several R functions behave differently depending on the type of object on which they act. As we saw earlier, the summary() function outputs descriptive statistics when it is given a vector. When given a data frame, it outputs summary statistics for each variable, as shown in the following code:

```
> summary(mydata)
     admit              gre             gpa
 Min.   :0.0000   Min.   :220.0   Min.   :2.260
 1st Qu.:0.0000   1st Qu.:520.0   1st Qu.:3.130
 Median :0.0000   Median :580.0   Median :3.395
 Mean   :0.3175   Mean   :587.7   Mean   :3.390
 3rd Qu.:1.0000   3rd Qu.:660.0   3rd Qu.:3.670
 Max.   :1.0000   Max.   :800.0   Max.   :4.000
```

R has many built-in functions for fitting statistical models. For example, we can estimate a linear regression model, that is, a model that predicts the level of a continuous variable with another continuous variable(s), by **ordinary least squares (OLS)** with the first two lines of the next code. Note that the tilde (~) in the following code is used to separate the left-hand side of the equation from the right-hand side of the equation. In this simple regression example, we are regressing y on x, or gre (mydata$gre) on gpa (mydata$gpa). When the summary command is used with a model as the argument, parameter estimates are displayed along with other auxiliary information. Finally, we present the regression example as a demonstration of a classical method in social science used on structured data. This book departs from these classical methods and structured data:

```
> mydata.model<- lm(mydata$gre~mydata$gpa)
> summary(mydata.model)

Call:
lm(formula = mydata$gre ~ mydata$gpa)

Residuals:
    Min      1Q  Median      3Q     Max
-302.394 -62.789  -2.206  68.506 283.438

Coefficients:
            Estimate Std. Error t value Pr(>|t|)
(Intercept)   192.30      47.92   4.013 7.15e-05 ***
mydata$gpa    116.64      14.05   8.304 1.60e-15 ***
---
Signif.codes:  0 '***' 0.001 '**' 0.01 '*' 0.05 '.' 0.1 ' '
```

One of R's great features is its extensibility. For instance, the `foreign` package allows users to import data formats other than those that R supports natively. To install a package, simply enter the following command in the terminal:

```
> install.packages("foreign", dependencies=TRUE)
```

The first argument to the function is the package name, and the second argument tells R to additionally install any other packages on which the one being installed is dependent. You will be asked to pick a mirror, that is, a location to download from. Choose one (it doesn't really matter which) and then input the following command to load the package:

```
> library("foreign")
```

To see all the different uses for this package, type `?foreign` as a command. One package that is particularly useful is the `sos` package, which allows you to search for other packages using colloquial search terms with the `findFn()` function. For example, when searching for a package that does non-linear regression, one could use the following command:

```
> library("sos")
findFn("non-linear regression")
```

Visualization in R

Visualization is a powerful tool for analyzing data and for presenting results. Many relationships and patterns that are obscured by summary statistics can be brought to light through visualization. The next graph shows a potent example of this. To begin with, let's look at some data that R comes with on the stopping distance of cars. This variable is contained in a dataset called cars, in a variable called **dist**. Histograms provide an informative way to visualize single variables. We can make a histogram with one line of code:

```
> hist(cars$dist)
```

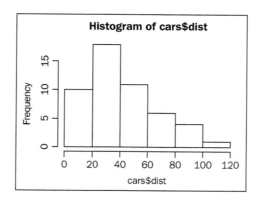

R makes the histogram, decides how to break up the data, and provides default labels for the graph title and the x and y axes. Type the `?hist()` command to see other arguments to this function that change the number of bars, the labels, and other features of the histogram.

Anscombe's quartet comprises four small datasets with two variables each. Each of the sets has similar mean and variance for both variables, and regressions of y on x in each dataset generate nearly identical regression estimates. Overall, we might be tempted to infer that these datasets are nearly identical. However, bivariate visualization (of the x and y variables from each dataset) using the generic `plot()` function shows otherwise. At a minimum, the `plot()` function takes two arguments, each as a vector of the same length. To create the following four plots, enter the following commands for each pair of x and y (x1 and y1, x2 and y2, x3 and y3, and finally x4 and y4):

```
# par can be used to set or query graphical parameters.
# subsequent figures will be drawn in a n-row-by-n-column array (e.g.
2,2)
#par(mfrow=c(2,2))
> plot(anscombe$x1, anscombe$y1, xlab="x1", ylab="y1",
  main="Anscombe 1")
> abline(lm(anscombe$y1~anscombe$x1)
```

The code discussed earlier shows how to create your own x and y axis labels and plot titles. The `abline` call adds straight lines to an existing plot, in this case, the best fit (or regression) line of y on x. The output of the previous code is shown as follows:

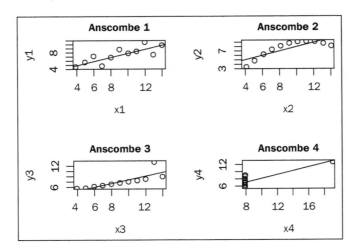

This exercise not only demonstrates some simple graphical commands, but also the importance of visualization generally. In later chapters, we elaborate on these graphical methods to enhance analyses and the presentation of analytical results.

Style and workflow

Statistical programmers can think of R code—like other languages—as being dysfunctional, functional but awkward, or graceful. Graceful code is clear and readable, which helps prevent errors. Here are a few tips on writing graceful R code:

- Filenames should end in .R and be meaningful.

- Variable names should be short. If necessary, use a period to delineate multiword variable names (for example, my.variable).

- Keep every line short. R will not terminate a command until all parentheses are closed, so feel free to wrap commands across lines for brevity.

- Use spaces before and after assignment, after commas, and around parentheses and operators (such as +) for readability.

- Use the left arrow with hyphen (<-) for assignment, never the single equals sign.

For more details on writing good R code, refer to the guide at http://google-styleguide.googlecode.com/svn/trunk/Rguide.xml. Again, though R can be used interactively from within the terminal, it is best practice to develop code within an IDE, such as RStudio, so that it can be saved, changed, and rerun. Additionally, building version controls and persistence into your code by storing it on GitHub may be important, especially if you find yourself working in a group environment. Finally, many users will find the creation of projects useful—the RStudio documentation offers useful tips on this topic.

Additional resources

This chapter provides what we hope is a useful, though necessarily brief, introduction to R. There are many resources available that will help you expand your R programming skill set. What follows is a short list of our favorites:

- *A First Course in Statistical Programming with R* by *Braun and Murdoch* (2007)
- *The R Cookbook* by *Teetor* (2011)
- Quick-R: http://www.statmethods.net/

Summary

This chapter has set out a case for using R, the statistical computing environment for data handling and analysis due to R's zero cost feature, flexibility, and large support community. By now, you've seen how to import, summarize, and visualize datasets as well as run and plot simple regression models. In the next chapter, we discuss how to obtain the social media source Twitter.

Mining Twitter with R

An obvious prerequisite to gleaning insight from social media data is obtaining the data itself. Rather than presuming readers have social media data at their disposal, we show them how to obtain and process such data. Specifically, this chapter lays a technical foundation for collecting Twitter data in order to perform social data mining.

Why Twitter data?

In this chapter, we introduce a technical foundation for mining social data. We do so through a set of examples that focus on Twitter data, though the analyses are equally appropriate for data from other venues. That being said, our use of Twitter warrants a bit more explanation: what's so interesting about Twitter?

One answer to this question is **nothing**. Twitter is one of several social media networks, and there is little reason to suspect that data from Twitter is fundamentally different from other socially generated data. Another answer is that Twitter is different in subtle but important ways. One distinction is Twitter's ability to foster second-order connections, or what *Granovetter* (1973-1983) calls **weak ties**. These weak ties are important as they bring information to individuals from those with whom they share less, thus dramatically increasing information exposure. Second, Twitter, perhaps more than some other social networks, allows users to self-organize. A third answer is that Twitter users actively use Twitter to gather insight, make recommendations, and lodge public complaints. The extent to which users find this information valuable gives credence to the notion of its validity.

Obtaining Twitter data

As expected, before analyzing Twitter data, one must obtain the data. One reason we like R for social media mining is that it makes obtaining targeted portions of Twitter data (relatively) simple. Besides having the capacity to read standard data types and files from traditional statistical software packages, R can also read many other specialized formats. For instance, R can read relational databases, Hadoop, and some web formats such as Twitter. This chapter first covers how to obtain Twitter data before describing some simple exploratory data analysis techniques.

To begin ingesting social media data from Twitter, you will need a developer account on Twitter. You can start one (free of cost) at https://dev.twitter.com/ apps. Once you have a Twitter account, return to that page and enter your username and password. Now, simply click on the **Create New Application** button and enter the requested information. Note that these inputs are neither important nor binding. You simply need to provide a name, description, and website (even just a personal blog) in the required fields.

Once finished, you should see a page with a lot of information about your application. Included here is a section called **OAuth settings**. These are crucial in helping you authenticate your application with Twitter, thus allowing you to mine tweets. More specifically, these bits of information will authenticate you with the Twitter **application programming interface (API)**. You'll want to copy the consumer key, consumer secret, request token URL, authorize URL, and access token URL to a file and keep them handy.

Now that we have set up an application with Twitter, we need to download the R package that allows us to pull tweets into our local R session. Though there are several packages that do this, we prefer the twitteR package for its ease of use and flexibility. Instructions for downloading packages can be found in *Chapter 2, Getting Started with R*, but in general, installing packages is done by invoking install. packages("..."). You can download the twitteR package and load it into your R session as follows:

```
> install.packages("twitteR")
> library(twitteR)
```

Now, we are just a few lines of R code away from pulling in Twitter data. If you are using a Windows machine, there is an additional prestep of downloading a cecert. pem file, which forms a portion of certain types of certification schemes for Internet transfers, as shown in the following code snippet:

```
> download.file(url="http://curl.haxx.se/ca/cacert.pem",
destfile="C:/.../cacert.pem")
```

In this example, we have saved the file to the `C:` directory, but you can save it to wherever you have the appropriate permissions on your machine. Also, note the use of the backslash instead of the Windows-standard forward slash in the file locations. Next, create R objects from your own consumer information, filled in here with xx to indicate a placeholder, as seen in the following lines of code:

```
> my.key <- "XX"
> my.secret <- "XX"
```

With that done, pass this information to a function called `OAuthFactory`. The `requestURL`, `accessURL`, and `authURL` in the following code snippet are demonstrative, but you should verify this information with that provided by Twitter as a part of authorizing your application:

```
> cred <- OAuthFactory$new(consumerKey=my.key,
    consumerSecret=my.secret,
    requestURL='https://api.twitter.com/oauth/request_token',
    accessURL='https://api.twitter.com/oauth/access_token',
    authURL='https://api.twitter.com/oauth/authorize')
```

Finally, input the `cred$handshake` call that follows this paragraph, including the full path to where you saved your `cacert.pem` file. This will bring up a URL in the R console that you will have to copy and paste into a browser. Doing so will take you to a Twitter page that will supply you with a numeric code that you can copy and paste into your instance of R after the `cred$handshake` call.

```
> cred$handshake(cainfo="C:/.../cacert.pem")
```

Finally, save your authentication settings as follows:

```
> save(cred, file="twitter authentication.Rdata")
> registerTwitterOAuth(cred)
```

The `registerTwitterOAuth` function returns a value of TRUE on success; you are now ready to begin mining Twitter data, and after all of these steps, it will seem very simple. The workhorse of the `twitteR` package is a function called, appropriately, `searchTwitter`. The standard arguments to the function are a search term, a number of tweets to return, and providing the `cacert.pem` file downloaded previously. More information about the function, including how to search specific time frames, geographic locations, and more, can be found by typing `?searchTwitter`. For now, let's pull in some tweets with the `#bigdata` hashtag and save them to an object called `bigdata` as follows (note that you may leave off the `cainfo` argument on non-Windows machines):

```
> bigdata <- searchTwitter("#bigdata", n=1500, cainfo="cacert.pem")
```

We can find out what class or type of object `bigdata` is by using the `class` function as follows:

```
> class(bigdata)
[1] list
```

We easily discover that `bigdata` is a list or a collection of objects. We can access the first few objects in a list using the `head()` function as follows:

```
> head(bigdata)

[[1]]
[1] "Timothy_Hughes: RT @MarketBuildr: Prescriptive versus #predictive
#analytics http://t.co/oy7rS691Ht #BigData #Marketing"

[[2]]
[1] "DanVesset: already have on my schedule 3 upcoming business trips
to #Texas .... where all data is #BigData"

[[3]]
[1] "imagineCALGARY: Excited to be working on our methodology for
turning #bigdata into the story of #yyc's #sustainability journey:
http://t.co/1zPMAEQIbN"

[[4]]
[1] "ozyind: RT @timoelliott: #BigData Will Save the Planet!!!
http://t.co/Tumfrse5Kc by @jamesafisher #analytics #bi #marketing"

[[5]]
[1] "BernardMarr: Mining Big Data For Sales Leads http://t.co/
Xh5pBGskaG\n\n#bigdata\n#datamining\n#analytics"

[[6]]
[1] "mobiusmedia: RT @carmenaugustine: One size does not fit all:
\"It's up to each professional to determine what they mean by #bigdata
#discovery\" @jaimefit…"
```

You can access a particular object within a list by using double braces as follows:

```
> bigdata[[4]]
[1] "ozyind: RT @timoelliott: #BigData Will Save the Planet!!!
http://t.co/Tumfrse5Kc by @jamesafisher #analytics #bi #marketing"
```

There is no guarantee that `searchTwitter` pulled in the number of tweets requested. We may have specified a small date range or an uncommon search term. Either way, we can check the length of the `bigdata` list-type object with the `length()` function as follows:

```
> length(bigdata)
1500
```

Before we get too search-happy, it should be noted that the Twitter REST API (v1.1) limits the number of searches that can be performed in any given time period. The limits vary based on the type of search, the type of application making the search, as well as other criteria. Generally speaking, however, when using searchTwitter, you will be limited to 15 searches every 15 minutes, so make them count! More specific information on Twitter's rate limits can be found at https://dev.twitter.com/docs/rate-limiting/1.1/limits.

The main tip to avoid the rate limit becoming a hindrance is to search judiciously for particular users, themes, or hashtags. Another option is to more frequently search for users and/or themes that are more active and reserve less active users or themes to intermittent search windows. It is best practice to keep track of your searches and rate limit ceilings by querying in R, or by adding rate limit queries directly to your code. If you plan to create applications rather than merely analyze data in R, other options such as caching may prove useful. The following two lines of code return the current number of each type of search that remains in a user's allotment, as well as when each search limit will reset:

```
> rate.limit <- getCurRateLimitInfo(c("lists"))
> rate.limit
   resource                 limit     remaining   reset
1  /lists/subscribers       180       180         2013-07-23 21:49:49
2  /lists/memberships       15        15          2013-07-23 21:49:49
3  /lists/list              15        15          2013-07-23 21:49:49
4  /lists/ownerships        15        15          2013-07-23 21:49:49
5  /lists/subscriptions     15        15          2013-07-23 21:49:49
6  /lists/members           180       180         2013-07-23 21:49:49
7  /lists/subscribers/show  15        15          2013-07-23 21:49:49
8  /lists/statuses          180       180         2013-07-23 21:49:49
9  /lists/show              15        15          2013-07-23 21:49:49
10 /lists/members/show      15        15          2013-07-23 21:49:49
```

To limit the number of searches we have to undertake, it can be useful to convert our search results to a data frame and then save them for later analysis. Only two lines of code are used, one to convert the bigdata list to a data frame and another to save that data frame as a comma-separated value file:

```
# conversion from list to data frame
> bigdata.df <- do.call(rbind, lapply(bigdata, as.data.frame))

# write to csv; fill in the … with a valid path
> write.csv(bigdata.df, "C:/…/bigdata.csv")
```

Preliminary analyses

Text data, such as tweets, comes with little structure compared to spreadsheets and other typical types of data. One very useful way to impose some structure on text data is to turn it into a document-term matrix. This is a matrix where each row represents a document and each term is represented as a column. Each element in the matrix represents the number of times a particular term (column) appears in a particular document (row). Put differently, the i, jth element counts the number of times the term j appears in the document i. Document-term matrices get their length from the number of input documents and their width from the number of unique words used in the collection of documents, which is often called a **corpus**. Throughout this book, we utilize the tm package to create document-term matrices and for other utilities. The following lines of code install the tm package, preprocess our list object, bigdata, and turn it into a document-term matrix:

```
> install.packages("tm", dependencies=TRUE)
> library("tm")

> bigdata_list <- sapply(bigdata, function(x) x$getText())
> bigdata_corpus <- Corpus(VectorSource(bigdata_list))
> bigdata_corpus <- tm_map(bigdata_corpus, tolower)
> bigdata_corpus <- tm_map(bigdata_corpus, removePunctuation)
> bigdata_corpus <- tm_map(bigdata_corpus,
    function(x) removeWords(x, stopwords()))
```

The first line uses a common family of functions (apply, lapply, and sapply). These functions, in general, deploy a function across a range of structured data. Sapply traverses a matrix, performs a function to retrieve text from the tweets, and turns the text into a list object, bigdata_list. The next line of code uses the Corpus function to turn the list of tweets into a corpus. A corpus is an abstraction in R to represent a collection of documents. The final three lines of code convert all of the words to lowercase, remove all punctuation, and drop stopwords, respectively. stopwords are very common words that do not carry much meaning, such as "a," "are," "that," and "the." A more complete list of stop words can be found at http://www.ranks.nl/resources/stopwords.html.

At this point, we can take a first look at our data using the WordCloud package, which, unsurprisingly, creates word clouds. Let's have a look at the following code snippet:

```
> install.packages("wordcloud")
> library("wordcloud")
> wordcloud(bigdata_corpus)
```

Now, let's go on to build the document-term matrix (or in this case, term-document matrix).

```
> bigdata.tdm <- TermDocumentMatrix(bigdata_corpus)
```

Simply calling the name of a term-document or document-term matrix pulls up some basic information about it, including the number of terms and documents, the number of non-zero (that is, non-sparse) cells, and some other information. Using the `findFreqTerms` function, we can access some of the most common terms in our matrix as follows:

```
> bigdata.tdm
A term-document matrix (532 terms, 99 documents)
Non-/sparse entries: 1024/51644

Sparsity           : 98%
Maximal term length: 18
Weighting          : term frequency (tf)

# identify terms used at least 10 times
> findFreqTerms(bigdata.tdm, lowfreq=10)
[1] "analytics" "big"     "bigdata"  "data"     "people"    "via"
```

We can also explore the data in an associational sense by looking at collocation, or those terms that frequently co-occur. From the previous list, "people" seems to be unexpected; so, we can explore the association of "people" and other terms in the corpus as follows:

```
> findAssocs(bigdata.tdm, 'people', 0.50)
2013     best     analytics
0.77     0.64          0.55
```

In the preceding code, each number is the correlation in the term-document matrix between the term it references and the word "people". Another way to get a visual sense of a set of documents is to cluster them. Clustering, in general, is a way of finding associations between items (for example, documents). This necessitates a measure of how far each observation is from every other one. Nearby observations are binned together in groups, whereas the ones further apart are put into separate groups. There are many ways to implement clustering; here, we use a variant called **hierarchical agglomerative clustering**. Interested readers can find out more about clustering methods at http://www.statmethods.net/advstats/cluster.html.

We implement our chosen method by first removing the sparsest terms from our term-document matrix. Sparse terms are those which only occur in a small proportion of documents. By removing sparse terms, we reduce the length of the term-document matrix dramatically without losing relations inherent in the matrix. The sparse argument in the following line of code details the proportion of zeroes a term must have before being considered sparse:

```
# Remove sparse terms from the term-document matrix
> bigdata2.tdm <-removeSparseTerms(bigdata.tdm, sparse=0.92)

# Convert the term-document matrix to a data frame
> bigdata2.df <- as.data.frame(bigdata2.tdm)
```

Next, we scale the term-document matrix because clustering is sensitive to the scale of the data used. Specifically, the scale function subtracts every element in a vector from the vector's mean and divides each element by the vector's standard deviation. Once scaled, we use the term-document matrix to compute a distance matrix, where each row is a document and each column is the same set of documents. Each cell represents the distance between each pair of documents.

```
# scale the data
> bigdata2.df.scale <- scale(bigdata2.df)

# Create the distance matrix
> bigdata.dist <- dist(bigdata2.df.scale, method = "euclidean")
# Cluster the data
```

```
> bigdata.fit <- hclust(bigdata.dist, method="ward")
# Visualize the result
> plot(bigdata.fit, main="Cluster - Big Data")

# An example with five (k=5) clusters
> groups <- cutree(bigdata.fit, k=5)
# Dendogram with blue clusters (k=5).
> rect.hclust(bigdata.fit, k=5, border="blue")
```

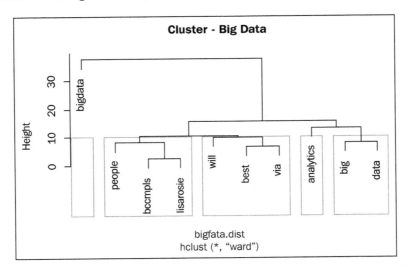

The preceding dendrogram shows our clusters in a tree diagram. The bottom row shows individual observations with groupings increasing in size as we traverse up the tree. Our sample was small and so our dendrogram is small, and our clusters may reflect groupings that do not generalize outside of our sample. For example, **bccmpls** and **lisarosie** reflect a conference (hashtag: bccmpls) in July 2013 where lisarosie was mentioned. This is mainly an artifact of our small sample and may not have been evident if we analyzed all Twitter data for 2013. Much less surprising is the clustering of **big** and **data**, both of which are closely related to analytics.

This chapter has laid the groundwork for the analysis of social media data. We have given you the tools to search, save, manipulate, and visualize social data. We urge readers at this point to go find and visualize some data for themselves before moving on to the next chapter.

Lastly, as a best practice, consider local- and cloud-based version control and code repositories. Both are great for professional, repeatable research and analysis efforts, and provide redundancy in the case of cloud-based version control systems. Git, GitHub, Dropbox, and Google Drive can all facilitate version control and code repositories. Git handles local version control and coupled with GitHub can move repositories to the cloud. GitHub stores data on the cloud (that is, remotely) to ensure that your code is preserved. Both Git and GitHub work well with RStudio. Dropbox and Google Drive offer only lightweight capability to do both version control and code repositories, but both are a bit more intuitive than Git. Understanding where your files are stored is a critical and often overlooked element in research and analysis. RStudio has some great mechanisms in place to manage files and projects. Whatever IDE you choose, learning more about managing data files, code, and plots are crucial to doing high quality work. In fact, these practices are so important that open source projects have been developed around this notion; one noteworthy example is ProjectTemplate (`http://projecttemplate.net`).

Summary

This chapter has provided an introduction to obtaining, manipulating, summarizing, and visualizing social media data. By now, you should be able to obtain Twitter data, save it, and store it locally in several formats. You should also be familiar with document-term matrices and several text exploration and visualization schemes. The next chapter discusses social media data from the perspective of social science research.

4
Potentials and Pitfalls of Social Media Data

Socially generated data, and especially social media data, comes with many complexities. Our ability to navigate these complexities as we describe and draw inferences from this data hinges on our thinking carefully about the potentials and pitfalls that arise in social media data. This chapter highlights some of the potentials and pitfalls of social media data.

Opinion mining made difficult

In this chapter, we highlight some of the potentials and pitfalls inherent in using social media data, and also in the tools we use to process it. These pitfalls are serious enough to warrant devoting an entire chapter to their enumeration and description. Though some of them cannot be ameliorated, we at least hope to give would-be analysts a fair warning so that they can enjoy their findings with an appropriately sized grain of salt.

In *The Empty Raincoat*, Handy described the first step to measurement as follows:

> "*The first step is to measure whatever can be easily measured. This is OK as far as it goes.*"

Twitter data is often used as the first step in measurement as it is easily obtained. University Professor and Princeton Fellow, Zeynep Tufekci (Tufekci, 2013), notes the danger in this practice using an analogy to the biological testing on Drosophila flies, better known as fruit flies. She points out that fruit flies are often used in laboratory settings because they are easy to breed and have simple life cycles. Tufekci cautions through a question: what if the fruit fly is systematically different than other organisms in ways beyond just their conveniently quick lifecycle? If so, the lessons learned from studying fruit flies may not generalize to other species. This would be doubly problematic because their ease of use causes them to be the focus of a preponderance of genetic and other research.

Similarly, Zeynep notes that Twitter may be a model organism, that is, model in the sense of a model plane, not in the sense of a model student. Twitter data and other social media data is accumulated quickly and is easily mined from various websites' APIs. The pervasiveness and perceived richness of these sources of data make them obvious choices for researchers seeking to take the pulse of the public. However, the ease with which this data can be obtained does not necessarily correlate with quality inferences. Similar to the data obtained from Drosophila flies, social media data may have limited generalizing ability due to the fact that social media users are often young, urban, and middle-class. This and other such caveats to the use of social media forms the focus of this chapter. Layered on top of these inferential concerns is the special requirement that we be sensitive to the privacy of social media users—just because they have made their thoughts public does not mean we should shine a spotlight on individuals, lest we misrepresent them. In addition to discussing the inferential challenges surrounding the use of social media, this chapter also sets down some fundamentals about sentiment extraction and measurement.

The conversation in the remainder of this chapter takes a social science tilt. We feel that this approach and this background is especially important given that important segments of the social data mining community are steeped in the workings of computers and algorithms. Even though this is the case, they may not have had an occasion to be introduced to measurement theory, descriptive and causal inference, and the many fallacies that can plague our best efforts at deriving insights from data.

Sentiment and its measurement

Fundamentally, this book is about measuring the sentiments of human beings expressed through social media. To further this aim, we pause to set forth a structured definition of sentiment and characterize some ancillary components of sentiments. A sentiment is a view or attitude towards a person, place, or thing. It is an opinion that is directed and often has a valence. For our purposes, we consider seven different factors surrounding a sentiment, expanding on the classic quintuple (5-part object). The classic quintuple includes the holder h that expresses the sentiment; the target of the sentiment, g; the sentiment itself, s; the polarity or magnitude of the sentiment, p; and the source of the data, c (as distinct from the source of the sentiment).

As an initial foray into sentiment analysis, we could analyze the sentence, "Mary thinks her new sneakers are really delightful." Mary is the holder or expresser of the sentiment *delight*. The target is obviously her sneakers, and the magnitude of her sentiment is strong or high as indicated by the adverb *really*. The source of this datum is the authors' imagination. In addition to these factors, we often find it useful to note the time and location of the expression of the sentiment, though these are absent from this example. The previous example's simplicity belies many extraordinary challenges in the field of sentiment analysis. Consider the following tweet:

> @<*username*> *I loooooooovvvvvveee my Kindle2. Not that the DX is cool, but the 2 is fantastic in its own right.*

The target of the sentiment is *Kindle2*, but a subtarget or the secondary target is Kindle DX; both are Amazon products and are viewed favorably. Kindle2 is loved by the user, but this is described atypically using *loooooooovvvvvveee* instead of love. Many sentiment analysis techniques rely on dictionaries, which may include love, but almost certainly not *loooooooovvvvvveee*.

Negation is also difficult to handle; consider sentences that include not, or more troublingly, not good or not bad. As we will see, negation can sometimes be partially captured by studying bigrams (two word pairs) instead of single words. This and other complexities serve to put something of an upper limit on the accuracy of our estimates of sentiment extracted from texts.

Not good and not bad negations complicate sentiment detection; intensification further compounds the difficulty of the task. Adjectives such as very, extremely, or hardly add or detract from the sentiment intensity. Superlatives form additional interesting cases such as "This wine is the most mediocre bottle I've ever purchased." Weighted terms in lexicons help mitigate negation and intensification, as does text scaling, discussed in *Chapter 6, Social Media Mining – Case Studies*.

Another example (Lui, 2012) that highlights further challenges is shown as follows:

> *"I bought a Canon G12 camera six months ago. I simply love it. The picture quality is amazing. The battery life is also long. However, my wife thinks it is too heavy for her."*

This example contains a sentiment that is broken up across subtopics within the overall review of the camera, some with positive valence and some with negative. This review is useful to depict the classic quintuple that defines sentiment analysis. Here, the source is the person expressing the opinion, the targets are the various subcomponents of the camera, and the sentiments about the various targets are "love", "amazing", "long", and "heavy." The source c refers to where the textual sentiment information was found, be it Twitter, a blog, or a sentence or article in a magazine.

The nature of social media data

The mechanical differences between blogs and/or consumer reviews and Twitter are obvious. Blogs and consumer review sites allow users to contribute finite but possibly large amounts of text data, whereas Twitter has a document length limit of 140 characters. While at first this may seem like a major limitation of Twitter data, in fact, it proves to be quite useful. When faced with this stark limit, users tend to be pithy and accurate rather than loquacious and artful. This brevity makes sentiment extraction much simpler than it is for longer documents; however, it comes with its own unique challenges.

Throughout this book, social media data, and especially Twitter data, will be examined in increasing detail and with increasing sophistication. In order to accomplish this aim, we first need to get a sense of some of the complicating factors involved in studying sentiments. The first factor might well be that sentiment is often nonhomogeneous. For instance, groups of people may be split in their opinions about a topic. In fact, a single person may hold conflicting views as well. However, trying to condense group-level or individual-level sentiments into a single numeric measure may obscure this heterogeneity. For instance, a group of people with neutral views on a topic and a group with two vehemently opposed subgroups would both score nearly zero (or neutral) on many additive scales.

Traditional versus nontraditional social data

We compare social media data with traditional social science data in an effort to provide context for its analysis. In this section, we also make readers aware of the general classes of pitfalls that affect any measurements or inferences drawn from data. The ultimate goal of this discussion is to set out a sound analytical framework as well as generate an awareness of the limitations of social data and methods. This is so that analysts can "measure (all) what is measurable, and make measurable (all) what is not so" (Galileo, 2008) responsibly.

Prior to the era of high-velocity data, computational social scientists relied on two sources of observational (that is, nonexperimental) data: they could hand-code it themselves or use large, slow-moving datasets collated by governments and organizations. Collecting one's own data is slow and costly. It involves interviewing experts and checking for reference sources. This type of data collection is also prone to errors due to differences between coders or within coders over time if the collection is ever done again. An alternative is to use data sources that are large but slow to change.

For instance, the United States Census Bureau serves as a leading provider of demographic and economic data. The Census Bureau compiles mountains of data with broad coverage and high accuracy. However, the Bureau's best known collection, the Census of Population and Housing, is only collected once a decade and is often not appropriate for the sophisticated questions that we have today.

These surveys have been crucial to social scientific research. The multivariate nature of this data provides rich sets of independent and dependent variables. However, the aggregate and infrequent nature of institutional data often results in pooled cross sections of randomly sampled individuals at different points in time. Rather than analyzing groups at discrete points in time, or aggregating them into heterogeneous bundles, social media data allows the possibility of tracking groups and individuals over time.

Social media is captured at the individual level and at an extraordinary rate. Their continuous nature over time and space makes them ideal for multivariate analysis and cross-correlation. Furthermore, aggregating social data often proves to be much simpler than attempting to disaggregate institutional data. Put differently, inferential challenges surrounding the study of individuals are much more easily overcome than those surrounding the study of groups. We explore these issues one by one in the forthcoming sections.

The conversation about social media data often becomes a conversation about Big Data and how Big Data is hard to analyze. While some are caught up in defining Big Data in terms of storage (too big to fit in a relational database) or analysis (too big to use standard maximum likelihood techniques), we find that these definitional points are less crucial than a deep understanding of the measurement and inferential challenges inherent in dealing with social media data.

Measurement and inferential challenges

Many of the activities that fall under the umbrella term of data mining involve either measurement or inference, or possibly both. This section details some of the challenges researchers face when attempting to measure difficult social science concepts or trying to infer general patterns from subpopulation sets of data. These tasks, measurement and inference, are often one and the same in the social sciences. While one can use a ruler to measure height, there is no way to directly measure sentiment or affinity. Instead, we create proxy measures for these concepts and hope to make accurate inferences about these quantities.

Overfitting is a common problem in social science research, especially in Big Data. The goal of many analyses is to quantify a relationship accurately. In an effort to do so, many researchers make a model of a particular dataset that fits that data very nicely. That is, the model explains a high proportion of the variation in the data at hand. These researchers often erroneously conclude that a model that fits their data well is a high-quality model. However, of crucial importance is how well they have captured the relationships in the data generally, not just in their small sample of data. A set of relationships that characterize a sample (also called training data) but do not fit other data of the same type or source (commonly referred to as test data) is said to be overfit. Though overfitting is a common problem in small data settings, researchers should be wary of it when using Big Data as well. To avoid overfitting, data miners ought to use parsimonious models and cross-validate their models on different data or subsets of their initial data. We discuss these methods throughout the book as examples of good practice.

Big Data further complicates a pair of issues that pose challenges in smaller datasets as well. The first is technically referred to as mixtures of relationships. In plain language, this refers to there not being one pattern in a set of data, but several possibly conflicting patterns. For instance, suppose a drug has a positive effect on men but a negative effect on women. An imprudent researcher might look for an effect of the drug and find zero effect, assuming about half of the data belongs to each gender. Here, a mixture of patterns mask each other. This challenge in data analysis is exacerbated by the large number of possible patterns in data that includes many variables and data that covers broad swaths of time, space, groups, and individuals. Identifying mixtures is often best done by exploring interactions between variables and by visualizing your data.

The second concern exacerbated by very large datasets is the recovery of findings that are statistically significant but substantively tiny. Many statistical techniques not only quantify relationships, say, between variables x and y, but also provide measures of the extent to which those relationships are unlikely to be zero. Relationships that are found to be unlikely to equal zero are said to be statistically significant. However, researchers should be aware of the fact that relationships can simultaneously be non-zero and trivially small. This is especially true in Big Data applications, because our ability to discriminate effect sizes from zero usually increases with data size. To avoid this pitfall, make sure to assess the substantive importance of any findings you generate, not just their statistical robustness. For instance, if you find an increase of 2 percent in consumer sentiment related to your product, would this increase, even if statistically robust, be important? To whom and why? What if the effect size was estimated to be non-zero, still only at 1 or 0.5 percent?

The **modifiable areal unit problem (MAUP)** is a source of statistical bias that comes in two flavors: scale and zonal problems. The issue was discovered by *Gehlke* and *Biehl* (1934) and described more completely by Robinson (1950) and Openshaw (1984), who lamented the following:

> *"The areal units (zonal objects) used in many geographical studies are arbitrary, modifiable, and subject to the whims and fancies of whoever is doing, or did, the aggregating."*

Openshaw and *Taylor* (1979) described how they had constructed all possible groupings of counties in Iowa into larger districts. When considering the correlation between percent of Republican voters and percent of elderly voters, they could produce a million or so correlation coefficients. A set of 12 districts could be contrived to produce correlations that ranged from -0.97 to +0.99. The modifiable temporal unit problem is the temporal companion of MAUP, but instead of geographic aggregation, the problem relates to temporal aggregation. To avoid finding spurious relationships when aggregating data, try to aggregate to a natural or substantively meaningful unit. Additionally, try aggregating to several units of varying sizes to ensure the robustness of your results.

Another concern stems from how you choose what data to analyze. When you build your sample based on the value of the variable of interest (that is, the dependent variable), you bias your study in a way that leads to low or even zero explanatory power. A toy example helps illustrate that if you want to study the factors that lead to business success, and thus examine 50 successful businesses and find that all 50 have CEOs that drive sports cars, you might conclude that this is a key cause of success. Obviously, such a study is flawed because of sampling of the dependent variable; to understand the causes of success, you would have to compare successful companies with unsuccessful ones. Though this seems obvious, even academic researchers fall victim to this error, such as the study of suicide terrorism done by *Robert Pape* (2003). Pape only looked at cases of suicide terrorism in an effort to make claims about the causes of suicide terrorism.

Self-selection is a constant concern in social science research. We must keep in mind that social data is volunteered by people, and that these people may not be indicative of the population generally. For instance, if we pull down geo-located Twitter data about President Obama, we must keep in mind that these tweets would almost entirely comprise users on Twitter (perhaps a young, upper-middle class group). This sample may not be representative of, say, likely US voters (whose modal member is older and middle class).

When interpreting our findings, we need to be careful not to fall victim to the ecological fallacy — the incorrect assumption that facts about about a group apply equally to members of the group. For example, if a researcher finds that men are more aggressive drivers than women, this does not imply that all men are aggressive drivers. Conversely, finding no relationship between income and infant mortality at the county or state level does not mean that there is no relationship between these factors at the household level. Ecological fallacy ought to be considered a special case of MAUP. In general, we can avoid these fallacies by making inferences only for the level of data that we have — inferences about groups from group-level data and inferences about individuals from individual-level data. Even more concrete advice is to try and match the level of data you collect with your research question of interest. For example, if you are studying household-level economic decisions, then attempt to capture household data!

As *Zeynep* (2013) astutely noted, social media mining and sentiment analysis often hinge on a plus one additive property where polarity is counted as the cumulative frequency of positive and negative words. However, not all words have equal impact, and some words scale differently than others. Later in this book, we discuss an unsupervised method that outlines this scaling problem and offers a solution.

The final pitfall we warn against is to watch out for dissimilar denominators that lead to intrinsic heterogeneity. This issue affects researchers who attempt to compare the sizes of different phenomena when a better measure would be a phenomenon's rate. For instance, if one tweet is retweeted 50 times and another is retweeted 100 times, upon first glance, we might be tempted to conclude that the second tweet was more interesting. However, what if the first tweet was only seen by a total of 100 people, while the second was seen by 10,000 people? Then, we could more accurately say that the first had a 50 percent retweet rate, while the second only had a 1 percent retweet rate. While the example makes it clear that the way to avoid dissimilar denominators is to pay appropriate attention to them, it is not always easy to obtain the appropriate denominator for any given metric.

Summary

Social data miners need to become more explicit in discussing, and where possible addressing, the pitfalls and assumptions that underpin their data and methods. Doing so will force researchers to be cautious and stay within appropriate inferential boundaries, while also allowing consumers of insights derived from social data mining to be aware of their limitations.

The upside of the model organism, Twitter, is that it provides a common, shared laboratory of interest that cannot be ignored by scientists, researchers, or practitioners; however, as was hopefully made clear in this chapter, harnessing it should be done with caution. Only through careful, thorough contemplation of the nature and structure of social data will mining provide us with answers to today's pressing social and human questions.

The last note we wish to make is that all data has shortcomings. Data is produced from an imperfect world, and we would therefore expect it to be imperfect. Regardless of whether your data is perceived to be from an authoritative source or not, one should still think in the terms outlined earlier. Measurement, reliability, validity, and potentials and pitfalls are pervasive considerations of data whether that data is small or big, good or bad, or traditional or nontraditional.

5
Social Media Mining – Fundamentals

Techniques used to extract sentiment from social media data are complex, at times counterintuitive, and often laden with assumptions. Before providing readers with a how-to guide to implement these models, we think it is critical to explain the techniques in depth so users can deploy them appropriately. This chapter explains the theoretical grounds for the techniques developed in the next chapter and serves as a bridge between the discussion of the pitfalls of social media mining and the execution of that mining.

Key concepts of social media mining

We find it useful to situate social media mining within the context of traditional social science research. While defining social science is difficult, Jean Anyon's perspective is a nice starting point. She suggests that socially explicit theory, and thus social science, should be empirically constructed, theoretically defensible, and socially critical. More generally, social science's main aims are to generate theories that explain individual-and group-level behaviors and then to examine the veracity of those theories with evidence. Generally, these theories are more valuable insofar as they allow a deeper understanding of human behavior, and especially so if they provide an understanding sufficient to allow for intervention. Our approach to social media mining strives to take this challenge to heart; thus, throughout this book, we use social media data to ask and answer questions of pressing social relevance.

Traditional social science not only focuses on important questions, but also seeks to uncover relationships that are interesting and unexpected. The world around us is full of complex social behavior; though identifying mundane facts is sometimes helpful in the name of basic research, it does little to help us understand social behavior. We take to heart the mandate to find interesting relationships as we mine social media data — a particularly complex and rich source.

At heart, however, social science is not a focus on the important or the interesting. It is science, which means that it is a set of methods and practices designed to generate and verify facts. The logic of science, regardless of whether it proceeds quantitatively or in a qualitative fashion, is fundamentally about knowledge discovery and accumulation. This logic helps mitigate several shortcomings in reasoning that frequently hinder our ability to make correct inferences. Some examples include illusory correlations (perceiving correlations that do not exist), selective observation (inadvertently cherry-picking data), illogical reasoning, and over or under generalizing (assuming that facts discovered in one domain apply to others as well). Generally, the scientific process helps avoid the discovery of false truths often arrived at through deduction, speculation, justification, and groupthink.

Good data versus bad data

Traditional social science data differs markedly from social media data in several respects. First and foremost, traditional social science data is most often collected in targeted and rigorous ways. For instance, the US census targets nearly the entire US population and has a strong methodology for attaining this target. Researchers interested in the sentiments of particular demographics can target them specifically through surveys or polls, and can additionally tune survey instruments to carefully elicit the information they desire.

The steep downside to these classes of data sources is that they are often extremely limited in their geographic or temporal coverage. As such, they do not allow for broad generalizations or comparisons across place and time. Broader surveys, such as the US census, capture information about a large number of people, but usually only capture cursory descriptive information. Furthermore, this information is captured infrequently and in ways that are incomparable across borders. Narrower surveys, such as those fielded by researchers and firms, obviously are limited in their ability to support inferences about broad populations.

These data sources, despite their shortcomings in terms of coverage, are held in high regard due to their focused and authoritative nature. These sources are used due to the fear that bad input data will yield low-quality inferences, or "garbage in, garbage out," as the saying goes. But, what is garbage data? Should we consider social media data garbage because of its unfocused nature? Also, under what circumstances might we be willing to use social media data?

Our view is that focused, purpose-collected data is the best option when it is available. This statement may come as a surprise in a book on social media mining, but the linchpin of the statement is the phrase *when it is available*. For the vast majority of emerging questions related to business, politics, and social life, purpose-collected social science data-sets simply do not exist. As such, we take the pragmatic position that social data, due to its broad coverage and large volume, makes a nice fallback to targeted data. Social data is bad in the sense that much of it will be inapplicable to any particular question; however, limited applicability is certainly better than utter absence of data. The reality is that we live in an imperfect world, which will consequently yield imperfect data. Our job, as data analyst is to work with data in responsible ways.

This book does not cover how to handle poor, dirty, missing, or incorrect data in a comprehensive manner. However, we do wish to promote the use of social media data and its utility in cases where traditional social science data-sets do and do not exist and where there are low and high barriers to targeted collection.

Traditional social science modeling techniques tend to require data-sets in which observations are independent of one another. However, data gleaned from social media outlets, such as Twitter, is almost certainly not independent. That is, data is not randomly sampled from a larger population and thus each observation is likely to be related to observations that are nearby in some sense. For example, tweets about a large public event arise around the same time and from the same area. Also, many may express similar views. This nonindependence has implications for how you handle tweets given their degree of centrality, shared geography, and repetition through retweets. Although we do not often study sentiment polarity explicitly in terms of networks, doing so may prove useful for future researchers. We anticipate research in that direction will produce better measures and predictions, localized lexicons, and other advantages.

Understanding sentiments

Social media mining can and should have broad interpretation. It is not the intent of the authors to confine social media mining to sentiments or opinions, but rather we suggest that a sentiment or opinion is a useful tool for many research pursuits.

Until recently, sentiment was understood as a ubiquitous and constant part of the human experience, with variations in sentiments changing only slightly up or down. Klaus Scherer (2000) developed a working definition as follows:

> *"Emotions (sentiments) are episodes of coordinated changes in several components in response to external and internal events of major significance to the organism."*

It is our intent to understand, measure, and interrelate these changes in a sentiment. Scherer's typology of emotions is a useful grounding point for the understanding of sentiments, and as a jumping-off point for a discussion of the difficulty in measuring sentiment-laden text.

Scherer's typology of emotions

Scherer's typology of emotions is briefly explained as follows:

- **Emotion**: This is a brief, organically synchronized evaluation of a major event, for example, being angry, sad, joyful, ashamed, proud, or elated

- **Mood**: This is a diffused, non-caused, low-intensity, long-duration change in subjective feeling, for example, being cheerful, gloomy, irritable, listless, depressed, or buoyant

- **Interpersonal stance**: This is an affective stance towards another person in a specific interaction, for example, being friendly, flirtatious, distant, cold, warm, supportive, or contemptuous

- **Attitude**: This is enduring, affectively colored beliefs or dispositions towards objects or persons, for example, being liking, loving, hating, valuing, or desiring

- **Personality traits**: These are stable personality dispositions and typical behavior tendencies, for example, being nervous, anxious, reckless, morose, hostile, or jealous

Generally, when we try to measure a sentiment, we talk about Scherer's emotions; though, in some situations, we might try to capture longer-term phenomena such as moods.

Anchoring the neo-social science approach using Twitter data versus other types of social media data is important as well because not all data is equal. Twitter data differs from data derived from sites such as Yelp and Google Reviews due to the simple fact that Twitter does not have ratings or explicit targets. If we want to know the sentiment of a given source or topic, whether it is the iPhone 5S or something more sensitive such as social policy, we have to discover that signal in a corpus of other signals. However, Yelp and Google Reviews (just two examples of many) have explicitly accounted for the source or topic by design and have ratings designed to measure sentiments.

A tweet is what Twitter users send to each other and to the Twittersphere. A tweet is sometimes a sentence and other times not, but it is restricted to 140 characters or approximately 11 words. Twitter therefore provides sentence-level sentiment analysis as opposed to reviews on Yelp or Google Review, which usually constitute the entire documents.

Sentiment polarity – data and classification

Social media mining primarily involves the following two steps:

1. Identifying and retrieving content related to the topic of interest.
2. Measuring the polarity of each datum.

The first step, message retrieval, requires some a priori insight into the topic of interest. The goal of message retrieval is to seek out only the messages or pieces of text that contain sentiment-laden content related to a particular topic. This topic could be almost anything of interest, subject to the constraint that information exists about it on public social media. For instance, in *Chapter 3*, *Mining Twitter with R*, we examined the topic Big Data, and in *Chapter 6*, *Social Media Mining – Case Studies*, we delve into social issues such as abortion and the economy. Atmospherics, that is, data gathered in an effort to track local sentiments with regards to economic, cultural, or political topics, can also be analyzed, as we do in *Chapter 6*, *Social Media Mining – Case Studies*. Lest readers think that social media is too diffuse to be useful, as of the writing of this book, at least one hedge fund uses atmospherics gleaned from Twitter to gauge stock prices.

To gather data, we generally collect content that contains a manually specified (set of) keyword(s). This is called the target. For example, the target for presidential approval would use the topic keyword **obama**. We may wish to add context to analyses done on particular keywords by adding additional opposing or specifying keywords. For example, in addition to **obama**, we could add **romney** to provide a counterpoint if we were studying the 2012 presidential election campaigns. Depending on the purpose of our analysis, we could jointly search for, say, **obama** and **economy** to target more specific subjects.

Topic models represent a second, more sophisticated, and potentially more thorough way of capturing bits of text that are relevant to a particular analysis. These models take very large sets of documents as their inputs and group them probabilistically into estimated topics. That is, each document is proclaimed to be a mixture of one or more topics that are themselves estimated from the data. This allows users to find texts that are related to a topic, though they may not explicitly use a particular keyword. The details of this class of statistical models are outside the scope of this text; however, in *Appendix, Conclusions and Next Steps*, we point readers to references on the theory and estimation of this exciting new class of tools.

Social data mining is the detection of attitudes, and the easiest way to understand it is through the following structure:

sentiment = {data source, source, target, sentiment, polarity}}

The parameters are explained in detail as follows:

- **Data source**: This relates to understanding the source of the data; that is, is the source a sentence or an entire document? Twitter or a blog?

- **Source or holder**: This is the one that expresses a sentiment or an opinion,

- **Target or aspect**: The target or aspect is what or to whom the sentiment is directed toward.

- **Type of sentiment**: This is the type(s) of emotion(s) expressed, that is, like, love, hate, value, desire, and so on.

- **Polarity**: These are juxtapositional sentiments on a dimension, that is, positive or negative.

The following examples highlight these components and also some of the challenges involved in sentiment analysis. We have parts of two reviews: one about *Steven Spielberg* and another about *John Carpenter*. In both examples, the data source is the **Internet Movie Database (IMDB)** that considers itself the world's most popular and authoritative source for movie, TV, and celebrity content. The holder is the one who wrote the review, and the targets are *Steven Spielberg* and *John Carpenter* respectively. However, the target is complicated by mentions of various movies over time. Also, complicating matters is the variety of sentiment types and polarities.

> *Steven Spielberg's second epic film on World War II is an unquestioned masterpiece. Spielberg, ever the student on film, has managed to resurrect the war genre by producing one of its grittiest and most powerful entries. He also managed to cast this era's greatest answer to Jimmy Stewart, Tom Hanks, who delivers a performance that is nothing short of an astonishing miracle for about 160 out of its 170 minutes; Saving Private Ryan is flawless, literally!*

> *There was a time when John Carpenter was a great horror director. Of course, his best film was 1978's masterpiece Halloween; however, he also made The Fog in the 1980s and 1987's underrated Prince of Darkness. Even, Heck made a good film, In the mouth of madness, in 1995. However, something terribly wrong happened to him in 1992 with the terrible comedy Memoirs of an Invisible Man.*

Supervised social media mining – lexicon-based sentiment

Lexicon-based sentiment classification is perhaps the most basic technique for measuring the polarity of the sentiment of a group of documents (that is, a corpus). Lexicon-based sentiment measurement requires a dictionary of words (a lexicon) and each word's associated polarity score. For example, a lexicon may contain the word excellent, which might have a score of positive two. Similarly, the word crummy may score negative one and a half. In the simplest implementation of lexicon-based sentiment analysis, all of the words in a document are compared to the words in the lexicon. Every time a word is used that is in the lexicon, the associated score is added to that text's overall sentiment score. For example, the sentence "I found the customer assistance to be excellent," would score a positive two.

A lexicon-based sentiment often entails merely counting the opinion words from a subset of data from a particular source. This approach certainly has errors, as does perhaps all natural language processing; however, in aggregate, the lexicon-based approach has proven to be fairly robust, even when only used on subsets. Additionally, there are many possible ways to aggregate the sentiment scores of each word, but most commonly, they are simply summed up to form an overall score for a document.

Despite lexicon-based sentiment classification being considered here as basic, it is still difficult. This is primarily due to the fact that when counting words with positive or negative valences, one must decide which words to count as each. Different dictionaries of positive and negative words can generate different sentiment scores for the same sentences. Some words with perceived sentiment are more neutral, while others have perceived neutrality, but are in fact more extreme. This challenge arises, in part, due to varied usages of words within and across contexts.

Preassembled lexicons are incredible resources and are applicable for a wide variety of problems — we use several in *Chapter 6, Social Media Mining – Case Studies*. Despite subtle differences, they are all good starting points, but they are just that, starting points and not end points. Rather than utilizing a preassembled lexicon indiscriminately, researchers should often develop lexicons that are sensitive to the domain they are analyzing. For instance, a lexicon that is useful for economic atmospherics (where moderate and stable are positive) may prove useless for examining political leanings. Preassembled domain-specific lexicons exist as well and two popular economic lexicons will be used later. There are many approaches to extending both generic preassembled lexicons as well as domain-specific preassembled lexicons, and we will describe two rather intuitive ones, dictionary-based lexicons, and corpus-based lexicons in addition to preassembled lexicons.

Both dictionary-based and corpus-based approaches augment preassembled lexicons in one of the following two ways:

- Using a dictionary (that is, synonyms and antonyms) to add keywords external to our corpus to enhance our preassembled lexicon(s)
- Using the corpus directly to add words already internal to our corpus that are keywords but are not accounted for by preassembled lexicons

Merging preassembled lexicons, dictionary-based lexicons, and corpus-based lexicons offers the best chance to successfully estimate sentiment.

The two approaches (dictionary and corpus) produce empirically constructed lexicons that seek to calibrate the underlying sentiment by adding to the preassembled lexicons. The intuition is words appearing in the complete collection of lexicons (preassembled, dictionary, and corpus) within our set of documents returned from a narrow topic (the search set) are more likely to objectively describe sentiment information. In the lexicon approach, it is sufficient to simply count the frequency of words from our lexicons with the set of documents returned from our topic of interest and sum the results over time, by space or by product. The next chapter outlines this process in detail and sums the results' set over time where the target is the US economy.

Supervised social media mining – Naive Bayes classifiers

Methods to extract sentiments from documents can be broadly classified into supervised and unsupervised approaches (semisupervised approaches are also available but are outside the scope of this text. Interested readers can consult Abney (2007)). Supervised methods are those that utilize data that has been tagged or labeled. In the parlance of statistics, these approaches utilize observations with both independent and dependent variables. For instance, the following Naive Bayes classifier approach involves a training dataset of documents that have already been scored as having positive or negative sentiment; a statistical model based on these forms the basis of scoring further documents. In contrast, unsupervised learning algorithms do not require a dependent variable to be provided. For instance, the IRT-based method described later in this chapter scales documents along a continuum of sentiments with no need to provide a labeled training set. Additionally, lexicon-based approaches mentioned earlier can also function without prelabeled observations.

The Naive Bayes classifier, in spite of its unfortunate name, turns out to be a highly useful tool for sentiment analysis. At the most general level, the Naive Bayes classifier is exactly that: a classifier. Classifiers are statistical tools that are used for, among other things, predicting which of two or more classes a new observation belongs to. In our case, we want to train our classifier to be able to distinguish documents featuring positive sentiment from those featuring negative sentiment (the two types or classes of interest). To do so, we feed the algorithm a large set of documents that are already coded as containing positive or negative sentiments about a particular topic. Then, if all goes as planned, we can pass new documents to the model and have it predict the direction of their sentiment, or valence, for us. The downside to this and other supervised techniques is having to handcode a sufficient set of initial training data.

So, where did the naive part of the name come from, and why is this method useful in spite of its self-assumed simplicity? The goal of any classifier is to determine which class or type a new observation belongs to based on its characteristics and previous examples from both types that we have seen before (that is, from existing data). Some types of classifiers can account for the fact that the characteristics we use for this prediction may be correlated. That is, if we are trying to predict whether an e-mail is spam or not by looking at what words and phrases the e-mail contains, the words easy and money are likely to co-occur (and are likely to be indicative of spam messages). The Naive Bayes classifier does not try to account for correlations between characteristics. It just uses each characteristic separately to try to determine each new observation's class membership.

The naive assumption that all of the characteristics of an observation are unrelated is always wrong. In predicting whether or not to extend a loan to an individual, a bank may look at their credit score, whether or not they own a home, their income, and their current debt level. Obviously, all of these things are likely to be correlated. However, ignoring the correlations between predictive characteristics allows us to do two things that would otherwise be problematic. First, it allows us to include a huge number of characteristics, which becomes important. This is because in text analysis, individual words often have predictive characteristics, and documents often contain thousands of unique words. Other models have a difficult time accommodating this number of predictors. Secondly, the Naive Bayes classifier is fast, thus allowing us to use large training sets to train a model and to generate results quickly.

Unsupervised social media mining – Item Response Theory for text scaling

The techniques set out earlier for scaling or classifying sentiments in texts are fairly robust; that is, they tend to work well under a wide variety of conditions such as heterogeneous text lengths and topic breadths. However, each of these methods requires substantial analyst input, such as labeling training data or creating a lexicon. **Item Response Theory (IRT)** is a theory, but will be used in this text to refer to a class of statistical models that rely on that theory, providing a way to scale texts according to sentiment in the absence of labeled training data. That is, IRT models are unsupervised learning models.

IRT models were developed by psychologists for scoring complex tests and were then picked up by political scientists who employ them for scaling legislators. We will briefly explain the legislative context as that will help readers build intuition over how models work when applied to scaling texts. Consider a set of V voters, such as US Senators, who, over the course of a year, vote on B bills. For simplicity, assume each voter can only vote **yes** or **no**. We could then put all of the data into a matrix, where each row represents a voter and each column a bill. Each cell then represents a particular voter's decision on a particular bill, that is, yes (1) or no (0). Now, we need to make two related assumptions. The first is that all or most of these voters can be described as lying along a single underlying continuum. The second more trivial assumption is that this position influences their votes, at least on some bills. With these assumptions in place, we can estimate a statistical model that describes the probability of each cell in our data matrix being a one or a zero. The model is a function of each bill's difficulty of being voted for (that is, how controversial it is), each voter's position on the underlying scale, and how strongly each bill is affected by voters' locations on the scale. Technically, we estimate a logistic regression as follows:

$$pr(y^{vb}=1) = logit(b1^b * x^v - b0^b)$$

Here, x is the scaled position of each voter (v), $b0$ is the difficulty of voting yes for each bill (b), and $b1$ is the degree to which each voter's position affects their proclivity to vote in favor of each bill (b). Positive values of $b1$ mean that voters to the right are more likely to vote in favor of a bill, and negative values of $b1$ mean that senators to the left are more likely to vote for a bill.

As you will see, we apply the previous assumption to the analogous case of text scaling. To do so, we create a matrix with rows representing authors or documents (instead of voters) and columns representing words or phrases, (instead of bills). Each cell represents whether or not a particular author used a particular word or phrase. We modify the previous assumptions: authors lie along a sentiment continuum, and their placement affects their pattern of word use. The first part of this assumption is limiting. We can only apply the method to sets of documents that are sufficiently narrow to be usefully described by a single underlying continuum, and that continuum must essentially be the sentiment we are trying to measure. The results of this analysis are a continuous scaled measure of author (or document) location (x) as well as estimates of the weights for each word or phrase ($b1$). This scaled measure of location (x) represents the author's sentiment towards the topic under study if the previous assumptions are met.

The IRT-based method described here has mixed properties. It requires no training data, little subject matter expertise to employ, is language agnostic (that is, could function on any language), and generates a quantitative (instead of merely a binary) measure of a sentiment. However, this model can only be applied to documents that are all about the same topic, can only estimate a single underlying dimension, can be slow to estimate, and is not guaranteed to converge.

Summary

In this chapter, we learned key concepts related to sentiment analysis. Sentiment was defined and difficulties related to its mining were covered. We then walked through the theoretical underpinnings of three different models for sentiment analysis. We intentionally separated the details of implementation from theoretical concerns in hopes of giving readers an appreciation for the methods, including their strengths and weaknesses.

The next chapter delves into the details of implementing the classes of models described earlier.

6
Social Media Mining – Case Studies

The importance of examples cannot be downplayed as they help us to understand and enhanced understanding often leads to subsequent improvement of our skills. While this chapter represents a sizable minority of the overall book, it also represents the proportion of time spent during modeling, that is, only a sizable minority. The previous chapters have established a solid groundwork of key concepts and foundational knowledge such that readers can now responsibly digest, comprehend, and execute the case studies discussed in this chapter. This pivotal chapter provides accessible material and tangible examples, including lexicon-based, supervised, and unsupervised approaches to sentiment analysis.

Introductory considerations

As promoted often throughout this book, social data mining can be about more than mere product reviews. This is not to suggest that these methods are used exclusively for marketing or business, nor that using these methods for such analyses is unimportant. It is merely an acknowledgment that our goals are largely about investigating socially critical issues, such as abortion, gun control, and immigration, or parts of issues broadly set within the health, economic, and political categories. These are perspectives that remain intrinsically important to the human condition and societal progress. To that end, we have intentionally chosen topics that are hard-hitting. Also, while we promote social media data, specifically Twitter, we also find utility in these methods on varied datasets, both big and small. Consequently, examples include data from the Web that is not from Twitter, and we simultaneously highlight nuances to consider when working with varied datasets. Furthermore, social data mining is often about Big Data, and R does a good job with large datasets, but size can become a consideration when working with real-world datasets.

When working with larger files, in general, you should consider the following:

- How large is your dataset?

  Generally, the number of rows and columns is a good estimation given the content in each cell, that is, numeric versus character.

- How much memory does your system have?

  You may want to avoid reading in data with file sizes greater than the memory available to you. As a rule of thumb, the overhead associated with reading data to memory, which is the default behavior of R, is about double. Therefore, if you estimate your data to be 3 GB, then the memory required is roughly 6 GB. Most computers now have 8 GB and even 16 GB of RAM, but if you do not have enough system memory, then some social media mining applications may be intractable.

- How many open applications do you have, and what are they?

  If you think you will be broaching the limits of your system, then you may want to consider closing applications or reading your data into memory at a later time.

- What is your operating system? Is it 32-bit or 64-bit?

  Some operating systems are more efficient, and having a 64-bit machine will allow increased access to memory.

We suggest you read the help page for `read.table` and `read.csv`; both offer simple mechanisms to gracefully handle larger datasets. `colClasses` is another option that should be considered. This option takes a vector whose length is equal to the number of columns in your table. By specifying this option instead of using the default we can tune R to load much faster since R will know in advance what the columns are and know their class. Also, by specifying the `nrows` argument we tune the internal memory usage. When R doesn't know how many rows it has to read it makes some rather crass estimations, and when it underestimates the memory demands, it allocates more memory. The constant allocations take time, and if R overestimates the amount of memory it needs, your computer will run out of memory. Even a mild overestimate for `nrows` is better than none at all.

Case study 1 – supervised social media mining – lexicon-based sentiment

The *Beige Book* (http://www.federalreserve.gov/monetarypolicy/beigebook), more formally called the *Summary of Commentary on Current Economic Conditions*, is a report published by the **United States (US) Federal Research Board (FRB)** eight times a year. The report is published by each of the Federal Reserve Bank districts ahead of the Federal Open Market Committee meeting and is designed to reflect economic conditions. Despite being a report published by the US FRB, the content is rather anecdotal. The report interviews key business contacts, economists, market experts, and others to get their opinion about the economy.

The *Beige Book* has been in publication since 1985 and is now published online. The data used in this book can be found on GitHub (https://github.com/SocialMediaMininginR/beigebook), as well as the Python code for all the scraping and parsing.

An example from the full report of the *Beige Book* (October 2013) is shown as follows, which will give you some idea about the nature of the content. The full report is an aggregated view from the 12 Federal Reserve Bank districts:

> *Consumer spending grew modestly in most Districts. Auto sales continued to be strong, particularly in the New York District where they were said to be increasingly robust. In contrast, Chicago, Kansas City, and Dallas indicated slower growth in auto sales in September.*

The *Beige Book* differs from Twitter in numerous ways: not everyone has the freedom to participate, the data points are not socially linked, and users cannot respond to one another directly. For our purposes, however, the most important difference is that the *Beige Book* contains paragraphs of information per document rather than being a collection of single sentences as is the case with Twitter.

For simplicity, the data has been collapsed over space. Other versions of the data include longer temporal ranges of the data and can be found on the authors' GitHub account (https://github.com/SocialMediaMininginR/beigebook). These datasets include disaggregated geographic views of reports by city and disaggregated views by topic. As the earlier quote (October 2013) indicates, and as intuition may suggest, the economic conditions in the US are nonstationary; that is, regional variation exists due to economic shocks affecting cities and regions that are similar either geographically or functionally. A more robust analysis of the data might include sentiment analysis by city and include neighborhood effects—we simplify the analysis here for expository purposes by omitting these complicating factors.

As we discussed in the previous chapter, a necessary requirement of lexicon-based approaches to measuring sentiment is to procure lexicons against which our data needs to be tested. There are many extant dictionaries that vary in terms of how they were generated (manually versus empirically) and their breadth (general or subject-specific). We use two preassembled lexicons and augment each with additions, one empirically induced from the corpus and the other dictionary-based. Our general opinion lexicon was created by *Hu* and *Liu* (`http://www.cs.uic.edu/~liub/FBS/sentiment-analysis.html`), and our domain-specific lexicon was created by *Tim Loughran* and *Bill McDonald* (`http://www3.nd.edu/~mcdonald/Word_Lists.html`). While one is domain-specific (*Loughran* and *McDonald*) and the other is for more general use (*Hu* and *Lui*), both lexicons offer broad utility for textual analysis, natural language processing, information retrieval, and computational linguistics.

Let's start by loading our data, sentiment function, and lexicons. The `https_function`, located on the authors' GitHub account (`https://github.com/SocialMediaMininginR/https_function/blob/master/https_function.R`), will load R files directly into your R session over HTTPS. This allows us to centrally store code and data and to make it available in a simple, verbatim manner. The code present on GitHub is shown as follows:

```
# Run the following code - (Breyal)
https_function <- function(url, ...) {
  # load package
  require(RCurl)

  # parse and evaluate each .R script
  sapply(c(url, ...), function(u) {
    eval(parse(text = getURL(u, followlocation = TRUE,
    cainfo = system.file("CurlSSL", "cacert.pem",
    package = "RCurl"))), envir = .GlobalEnv)
  })
}
```

It should be noted that when performing this analysis, several tabs were used in RStudio. If you are using RStudio for the first time, you may want to consider how to make best use of the tabs for general organization. The following R code will appear to be all in one block, but in practice, the material was organized in three tabs in RStudio: one labeled **environment** that loaded packages and set working directories, a second tab that loaded the data named **load** (the labeling should be simple and sensible to you), and a third tab for **analysis**, which, as you may have guessed, is where most of the work was done. You can imagine extra tabs for data cleaning/munging code, another for visualization code, and maybe others. It is probably a bad idea to go beyond four or five tabs as the management of the tabs alone then becomes more of a task than what they are attempting to alleviate.

In the next section, we will pull in data from GitHub. In the event that you have trouble, we encourage you to go directly to GitHub and download the data (`https://github.com/SocialMediaMininginR`):

1. Load the `sentiment` function located at `https://github.com/SocialMediaMininginR`.

2. Load `https_function` located at `https://raw2.github.com/SocialMediaMininginR/sentiment_function/master/sentiment.R`.

The sentiment function is based on the approach of *Jeffrey Breen*. Some of his material is available on his blog at `http://jeffreybreen.wordpress.com/2011/07/04/twitter-text-mining-r-slides/`, and his complete code is available on GitHub at `https://github.com/jeffreybreen/twitter-sentiment-analysis-tutorial-201107`.

The `qdap` package in R has a polarity function based on the work of *Jeffery Breen*. Its goal is quantitative discourse analysis of transcripts containing discourse. The analysis in this first case study is designed to capture discourse by matching and then counting opinionated words based on our lexicons. The counting occurs by whole numbers and does not represent a scale. The `qdap` package ranks sentiment from -1 to 1, akin to text scaling of sorts. Breen's original work is used in the first case study over the `qdap` package since we promote a non-dictionary-based, unsupervised text scaling method in the third case study.

In the first case study, we are interested in determining economic conditions over time. The example captures opinions of experts and local businesses eight times a year. Sentiment analysis will give us insight into the strength and direction of those opinions. Again, to measure the opinions, we need lexicons to match against. Exactly which lexicon you choose to employ may have a direct impact on the analysis of opinionated text, so choose wisely and understand the lexicon landscape. As a rule of thumb, start with general preassembled lexicons; proceed to domain-specific preassembled lexicons; and lastly, advance to empirically constructed lexicons.

Next, we load our lexicons directly from GitHub as follows:

```
# Download positive lexicons from the Social Media Mining Github
account
# note: you will substitute your directory for destination file
locations
# On Windows machines you may have to disregard the method argument
> download.file("https://raw2.github.com/SocialMediaMininginR/neg_
words/master/negative-words.txt", destfile = "/your-localdirectory/
neg_words.txt", method = "curl")
```

```
> download.file("https://raw.github.com/
SocialMediaMininginR/pos_words/master/      LoughranMcDonald_pos.csv",
destfile = "/
your-localdirectory/          LoughranMcDonald_pos.txt",
 method = "curl")

# import positive lexicons from your local directory defined in
earlier step
> pos<- scan(file.path("your-localdirectory",
 'pos_words.txt'), what = 'character',
  comment.char = ';')

# import financial positive lexicon from your local directory defined
in earlier step
> pos_finance<- scan(file.path("your-localdirectory",
'LoughranMcDonald_pos.txt'),
  what = 'character', comment.char = ';')

# combine both files into one
> pos_all<- c(pos, pos_finance)

# Download negative lexicons from Social Media Mining Github account
# note: you will substitute your directory for destination file
locations
# On Windows machines you may have to disregard the method argument >
download.file("https://raw2.github.com/SocialMediaMininginR/neg_words/
master/negative-words.txt", destfile = "/your-localdirectory/pos_
words.txt", method = "curl")

> download.file("https://raw.github.com/
SocialMediaMininginR/neg_words/master/LoughranMcDonald_neg.csv",
destfile = "/your-localdirectory/LoughranMcDonald_neg.txt", method =
"curl")

# import negative lexicons from your local directory defined in
earlier step
> neg<- scan(file.path("/your-localdirectory/
", 'neg_words.txt'),
what = 'character',          comment.char = ';')

# import financial negative lexicon from your local directory defined
in earlier step
> neg_finance<- scan(file.path("/your-localdirectory/",
```

```
'LoughranMcDonald_neg.txt'),
  what = 'character', comment.char = ';')
# combine both files into one
> neg_all<- c(neg, neg_finance)


# Import Beige Book data from Github and create a new data frame.
# *Important* You have three options when ingesting Beige Book data.
   # beigebook_summary.csv is three years of data (2011 - 2013)
   # bb_full.csv is sixteen years of data (1996 - 2011)
   # BB_96_2013.csv is eighteen years of data (1996 - 2013)
# The example below uses beigebook_summary and bb_full
   # Feel free to ingest what you wish or try all three
   # Outputs will look different depending on the file you chose
> download.file("https://raw.github.com/
SocialMediaMininginR/beigebook/master/beigebook_summary.csv", destfile
= "/
your-localdirectory/BB.csv", method = "curl")


> BB <- read.csv("/your-localdirectory/BB.csv")
```

We now have data (*Beige Book*) and both of the lexicons, general and domain-specific, loaded into our R session as well as our sentiment function. Thus, we can begin some exploratory analysis to better understand the data. By using `colnames` on our `data. frame (BB)`, we identify the column names of BB. Other operations too give us a more complete examination of the *Beige Book*, such as `class(BB)`, `str(BB)`, `dim(BB)`, and `head(BB)`. An example of using `colnames` is shown as follows:

```
> colnames(BB)
[1] "year""month""text"
```

We can also check for missing data (year ~ month) using *Hadley Wickham*'s `reshape` package. We can see that there seems to be some systematic missing data, notably that May (5) and December (12) are missing data in all three years of data collection as shown in the following example:

```
> cast(BB, year ~ month, length)


year    1 2 3 4 6 7 8 9 10 11
1 2011 1 0 1 1 1 1 0 1  1  1
2 2012 1 1 0 1 1 1 1 0  1  1
3 2013 1 0 1 1 1 1 0 0  0  0
```

In the real world, data analysis is dirty. Consequently, most of your time will be spent on cleaning the data. Identifying missing data is central to that pursuit. The is.na() function in R helps identify missing data. Regular expressions too are pretty handy and aid in pattern matching by finding and replacing data. If you are unfamiliar with regular expressions, we suggest that you learn more; RegexOne has a great regular expression tutorial (www.regexone.com), and Debuggex Beta has a helpful debugger (https://www.debuggex.com/). An example of regular expressions is given as follows:

```
> bad <- is.na(BB)
# create a new object "bad" that will hold missing data, in this case
from BB.
> BB[bad]
# return all missing elements


character(0)
# returns zero missing elements. Alternately, adding !before "bad"
# will return all good elements.


# regular expressions help us clean our data
# gsub is a function of the R package grep and replaces content that
matches our search
# gsub substitutes punctuation (must be surrounded by another set of
square brackets)
# when used in a regular expression with a space â€~ â€~
> BB$text<- gsub('[[:punct:]]', ' ', BB$text)
# gsub substitutes character classes that do not give an output such
as feed, backspace and tabspaces with a space ' '.
> BB$text<- gsub('[[:cntrl:]]', ' ', BB$text)
# gsub substitutes numerical values with digits of one or greater with
a space ' '.
> BB$text<- gsub('\\d+', ' ', BB$text)
# we are going to simplify our data frame and keep the clean text as
well as keep both
# year and a concatenated version of year/ month/day and will format
the latter.
> BB.text <- as.data.frame(BB$text)
> BB.text$year<- BB$year
> BB.text$Date <- as.Date( paste(BB$year, BB$month, BB$day, sep = "-"
)  , format =   "%Y-%m-%d" )
> BB.text$Date <- strptime(as.character(BB.text$Date), "%Y-%m-%d")
> colnames(BB.text) <- c("text", "year", "date")
> colnames(BB.text)
[1] "text" "year" "date"
```

To perform a more complete exploration and refine our analysis, we may also create a corpus via `VectorSource`, which is present in the `tm` package. It is quite useful and can create a corpus from a character vector. A corpus is a collection of text documents. Our goal here is to revisit our data frame to perform our sentiment analysis, but in the meantime we require a more comprehensive understanding of our data, especially to augment our lexicons. In order to do so, we will work with our data as a corpus and term-document matrix using the `tm` package.

For example, we can create a corpus by combining two character strings into the `example_docs` object and convert it using `VectorSource` into a corpus as follows:

```
example_docs<- c("this is an useful example", "augmented by another
useful example")
> example_docs
[1] "this is an useful example""augmented by another useful example"

> class(example_docs)
[1] "character"

> example_corpus<- Corpus(VectorSource(example_docs))
> example_corpus
A corpus with 2 text documents
```

We can perform much of the same cleaning of the data using the `tm` package, but our data then needs to be in a corpus, whereas regular expressions work on character vectors as shown in the following code:

```
> install.packages("tm")
> require(tm)
> bb_corpus<- Corpus(VectorSource(BB.text))
# tm_map allows transformation to a corpora.
# getTransformations() shows us what transformations are available via
the tm_map function
> getTransformations()
   "as.PlainTextDocument" "removeNumbers"         "removePunctuation"
"removeWords"            "stemDocument" "stripWhitespace"
> bb_corpus<- tm_map(bb_corpus, tolower)
> View(inspect(bb_corpus))


# before cleaning:
"The manufacturing sector continued to recover across all Districts."
(2011,1)
# after cleaning:
"the manufacturing sector continued to recover across all districts"
(2011,1)
```

Stemming is rather useful for reducing words down to their core element or stem, as we show in the Naive Bayes and IRT examples. An example of stemming for the words stemming and stems would be stem — effectively dropping the -ing and -s suffixes, as shown in the following code:

```
# stemming can be done easily
# we just need the SnowballC package
> install.packages("SnowballC")
> require(SnowballC)
> bb.text_stm<- tm_map(bb_corpus, stemDocument)
```

When exploring our corpus, it is often important to accentuate the signal and reduce noise. We can accomplish this by removing frequently used words (such as *the*) commonly known as stop words. These commonly used words often have information value at or very close to zero.

We will use a standard list of stop words and augment this further with words specific to our corpus. The list of stop words started with a simple list generated by reading a few of the reports, but was expanded based on some text mining explained later. Again, the goal is eliminating words that lack discriminatory power. The cause for eliminating city names is due to their frequency of use as shown in the following example:

```
# Standard stopwords such as the "SMART" list can be found in the tm
package.
> stnd.stopwords<- stopwords("SMART")
> head(stnd.stopwords)
> length(stnd.stopwords)
[1] 571


# the standard stopwords are useful starting points but we may want to
# add corpus-specific words
# the words below have been added as a consequence of exploring BB
# from subsequent steps
> bb.stopwords<- c(stnd.stopwords, "district", "districts",
"reported", "noted", "city", "cited",   "activity", "contacts",
"chicago", "dallas", "kansas", "san", "richmond", "francisco",
"cleveland", "atlanta", "sales", "boston", "york", "philadelphia",
"minneapolis", "louis",   "services","year", "levels", " louis")
```

The bb.stopwords list is a combination of stnd.stopwords and our custom list discussed earlier. You can certainly imagine another scenario where these city names are kept and words associated with city names are examined. For the following analysis, however, they were dropped:

```
> length(bb.stopwords)
[1] 596
```

```
# additional cleaning to eliminate words that lack discriminatory
power.
# bb.tf will be used as a control for the creation of our term-
document matrix.
> bb.tf <- list(weighting = weightTf, stopwords  = bb.stopwords,
  removePunctuation = TRUE,
  tolower = TRUE,
  minWordLength = 4,
  removeNumbers = TRUE)
```

A common approach in text mining is to create a term-document matrix from a corpus. In the `tm` package, the `TermDocumentMatrix` and `DocumentTermMatrix` classes (depending on whether you want terms as rows and documents as columns, or vice versa) employ sparse matrices for corpora as shown in the following code:

```
# create a term-document matrix
> bb_tdm<- TermDocumentMatrix(bb_corpus, control = bb.tf)
```

```
> dim(bb_tdm)
[1] 1515    21
> bb_tdm
  A term-document matrix (1515 terms, 21 documents)

  Non-/sparse entries: 5441/26374
  Sparsity           : 83%
  Maximal term length: 18
  Weighting: term frequency (tf)
```

```
> class(bb_tdm)
[1] "TermDocumentMatrix""simple_triplet_matrix"
```

```
# We can get all terms n = 1515
> Terms(bb_tdm)
```

A good exploratory step to get a handle on your dataset is sorting frequent words. This helps to first remove stop words that lack discriminatory power as a consequence of their repeated use.

```
> bb.frequent<- sort(rowSums(as.matrix(bb_tdm)), decreasing = TRUE)
```

```
# sum of frequent words
> sum(bb.frequent)
```

```
[1] 8948

# further exploratory data analysis
> bb.frequent[1:30]
  # BEFORE removing stopwords
  chicago       demand       dallaskansas       san
  248           245          244                236
220
  richmond francisco      sales       cleveland atlanta
  218          217                    210       201
198
  boston york philadelphia minneapolis louis
  186         185          173                   154
140
  increased      growth     services    conditions      prices
  133            108        101         98
92
  mixed      continued      strong         home      manufacturing
  87         84             71             68                  68
  loan       steady         firms       construction   remained
  66         65             64          61
61

> bb.frequent[1:30]
  # AFTER removing stopwords
  demand       increased     growth    conditions     prices
mixed
  252          133           110       102
94            88
  continued        strong       loan      manufacturing
reports          home
  85               72           70        69
69               68
  steady       construction     firms       report      remained
consumer
  67           66               65          64
61               58
  increases        hiring     increase    production   residential
retail
  58               57         57          57
56               56
```

The word demand is a prominent noun, as are growth, conditions, and prices.
Prominent adjectives include mixed, strong, and steady, while prominent
verbs include increased, continued, remained, and hiring. It is too soon to
determine the general direction of opinion relating to the economy based on this
decontextualized information, but it does help us determine the nature of our corpus.

Finding the most frequent words (for example, *n*, where *n* is the minimum frequency) will help us build out our positive and negative library of words in order to refine our analyses and learn more about our corpus. This is the lexicon approach. A word such as `strong` would appear to be a good predictor of positive sentiment. Exploring the corpus itself can allow our lexicon to grow inductively, allowing us to augment our domain-specific dictionary or build one from a general purpose dictionary. The `any` function returns logical vectors if at least one of the values is true. Using the results from the frequent words, we can begin to test for the presence of words from within our corpus and our lexicons as follows:

```
# look at terms with a minimum frequency
> findFreqTerms(bb_tdm, lowfreq = 60)
 [1] "conditions""construction""continued""demand""firms"
 [6] "growth""home""increased""loan""manufacturing"
[11] "mixed""prices""remained""report""reports"
[16] "steady""strong"
```

Additionally, we could augment this even further by using a dictionary (for example, `http://www.merriam-webster.com`) to find words to add to our lexicon. The Thesaurus website is a good choice as it gives many relevant matches (`http://thesaurus.com/browse/increase`) and suggests hike, development, expansion, raise, and surge. These words may be useful. Also useful are their antonyms, which may be used in our negative lexicon. Words such as decrease, drop, shrinkage, and reduction may all prove to be helpful—none of which were included in the default lexicons nor in our manual additions to them. An example of using positive and negative words is shown as follows:

```
# Let us add some of these positive words:
> pos.words<- c(pos_all, "spend", "buy", "earn", "hike", "increase",
"increases",  "development", "expansion", "raise", "surge", "add",
"added", "advanced", "advances",  "boom", "boosted", "boosting",
"waxed",  "upbeat", "surge")

# And add the negative ones:
> neg.words = c(neg_all, "earn", "shortfall", "weak", "fell",
"decreases", "decreases",  "decreased", "contraction", "cutback",
"cuts", "drop", "shrinkage", "reduction",  "abated", "cautious",
"caution", "damped", "waned", "undermine", "unfavorable",  "soft",
"softening", "soften", "softer", "sluggish", "slowed", "slowdown",
"slower",  "recession")
> any(pos.words == "strong")
[1] TRUE
# TRUE is returned. Meaning, "strong" is already in our lexicon.
> any(pos.words == "increases")
[1] FALSE
# FALSE is returned.
# Meaning, "increases" is not already in our lexicon.
```

The word "increases" is not in our lexicon. The implications about the economy and its direction make this word potentially useful. Certainly, it could be associated with increases in unemployment; however, after reading a couple of the mentions of "increases", it seems a better predictor of positive sentiment. It seems the Federal Bank uses "decreases" to suggest negative direction.

We may want to find associations (that is, terms with correlations greater than 0.5) or correlations with various keywords, such as demand. This exploratory process can be used to augment our dictionary and also the contextualized local relationships of our data. We can get a general sense about the interaction between nouns (n) and verbs (v), such as the interaction between demand (n) and hiring (v) as well as material (n) and building (v) in the following example:

```
# interestingly, demand is associated with "weak"
> findAssocs(bb_tdm, "demand", 0.5)
    makers       season      products       weak         wood
years
    0.73         0.69         0.65         0.64
0.63         0.63
    livestock    category     pointed     december     electronic
feeding
    0.62         0.60         0.60         0.59
0.59         0.59
    november     power        snow       consistent     exceeded
manufacturers
    0.59         0.59         0.59         0.57
0.57         0.57


# "increased" is associated with "materials", "hiring" and "building"
> findAssocs(bb_tdm, "increased", 0.5)
    availability  materials   corporate     finding      qualified
hiring
    0.75         0.75         0.68         0.65
0.65         0.63
    selective    yields      purchases    building      dealers
side
    0.58         0.56         0.55         0.54                     0.54
0.51


# "growth" is associated with "slowdown" and "reductions"
> findAssocs(bb_tdm, "growth", 0.5)
    slowdownipo   reductions    capital      driven
    0.63          0.59          0.59          0.55
0.55
```

inputs	semiconductors	supplier	contributed	months
0.55	0.55	0.55	0.54	
0.54				
restrained	tax			
0.54	0.52			

Another potential step in our exploration of the data is to make a word cloud, which is a graphic that depicts common words in a corpus by displaying their relative frequencies as relative sizes. Word clouds give a sense of diction within our corpus. We utilize the `wordcloud` function from the `wordcloud` package to generate the useful graphic that is shown after the following code:

```
# Remove sparse terms from term document matrix with
# a numeric value of .95; representing the maximal allowed sparsity.
> BB.95 <- removeSparseTerms(bb_tdm, .95)

# Here we are sorting and counting the row sums of BB.95
> BB.rsums <- sort(rowSums(as.matrix(BB.95)), decreasing=TRUE)

# We will need to create a data frame with the words and their
frequencies.
> BBdf.rsums <- data.frame(word=names(BB.rsums), freq=BB.rsums)
> colnames(BBdf.rsums)
# [1] "word" "freq"

# Install RColorBrewer for coloring our wordcloud
> install.packages("RColorBrewer")
> require(RColorBrewer)

# RColorBrewer creates nice looking color palettes
# Create a palette, blue to green, and name it palette using brewer.
pal
> palette <- brewer.pal(9, "BuGn")
> palette <- palette[-(1:2)]
> install.packages("wordcloud")
> require(wordcloud)

# Create a png and define where it will be saved and named
> png(filename="your/file/location/name.png")
# Create a wordcloud and define the words and their frequencies as
well as how those word sizes will scale.
> bb_wordcloud <- wordcloud(BBdf.rsums$word, BBdf.rsums$freq,
> scale=c(7,.2), min.freq=4, max.words=200,
  random.order=FALSE, colors=palette)
```

```
# dev.off will complete the plot and save the png
> dev.off()
```

Word cloud

As you can see in the previous screenshot, **demand** and **prices** are central. Within the field of economics, demand has a nuanced and important meaning. Demand offers insight into the willingness to buy goods or a service.

You can imagine businesses and government alike spending a great deal of effort trying to understand the quantum of demand that exists within the public sector. Understanding this incorrectly or incompletely will result in incorrectly estimating the impact of government programs or, from a private sector perspective, will result in the loss of money or unrealized gains.

We are now in a position to run our data frame against the `score.sentiment` function. We will show results for the three and sixteen year datasets. Both datasets and the code for both analyses are located on GitHub:

```
# using our score.sentiment function on BB.text$text against pos.words
and neg.words
```

```
# progress = 'text' is useful for monitoring scoring of large
documents
# keep date and year since they are dropped in the score.sentiment
output
> BB.keeps <- BB.text[,c("date", "year")]
# run score.sentiment on our text field using pos.words and neg.words
> BB.score<- score.sentiment(BB.text$text, pos.words, neg.words,
.progress = 'text')
# add back BB.keeps to BB.score
> BB.sentiment <- cbind(BB.keeps, BB.score)
# colnames(BB.sentiment shows that we kept "text", "date", and "year"
field as well as the # new column "score"
> colnames(BB.sentiment)
[1] "date"    "year"    "score"     "text"
```

By examining BB.sentiment$score (the three year dataset), we discover a mean of 33. In other words, most scores are already above zero, suggesting that the sentiment is positive, but thereby making interpretability difficult. To improve interpretability, we mean-center our data and shift our midpoint value from 33 to zero. The new, empirically adjusted center may be interpreted as an empirically neutral midpoint. The histograms shown after the following code display both raw scores and centered scores:

```
# calculate mean from raw score
> BB.sentiment$mean <- mean(BB.sentiment$score)
# calculate sum and store it in BB.sum
> BB.sum <- BB.sentiment$score
# center the data by subtracting BB.sum from BB.sentiment$mean
> BB.sentiment$centered <- BB.sum - BB.sentiment$mean
# we can label observations above and below the centered values with 1
# and code N/A values with 0
> BB.sentiment$pos[BB.sentiment$centered>0] <- 1
> BB.sentiment$neg[BB.sentiment$centered<0] <- 1
> BB.sentiment[is.na(BB.sentiment)] <- 0
# we can then sum the values to get a sense of how balanced our data.
> sum(BB.sentiment$pos)

[1] 673
> sum(BB.sentiment$neg)
[1] 683
# we can create a histogram of raw score and centered score to see the
# impact of mean centering
```

```
> BB.hist <- hist(BB.sentiment$score, main="Sentiment Histogram",
xlab="Score", ylab="Frequency")
> BB.hist <- hist(BB.sentiment$centered, main="Sentiment Histogram",
xlab="Score", ylab="Frequency")
```

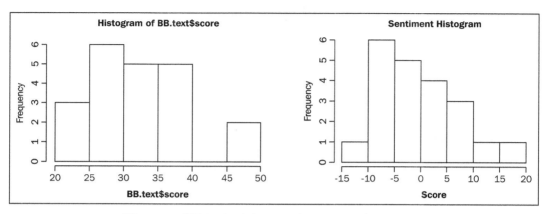

Histogram of BB.sentiment$score and BBsentiment$meancenter

Some of the upcoming plots will use a package named ggplot2, created by *Hadley Wickham*. Though difficult to master, ggplot2 offers some rather elegant and powerful graphing. This package is different from the package used for plotting in *Chapter 2, Getting Started with R,* and is shown here to offer diversity in the ways in which you may plot graphics. There are some rather good resources available if you are interested in learning more about ggplot2, but *The Grammar of Graphics* by *Leland Wilkinson* may be the most comprehensive:

```
# install and load ggplot2
install.packages("ggplot2")
require(ggplot2)
# using the results from the function to score our documents we create
# a boxplot to examine the distribution of opinion relating to
# economic conditions the labeling assumes here that you imported
# summary file of three years
> BB.boxplot<- ggplot(BB.sentiment, aes(x = BB.sentiment$year,
  y = BB.sentiment$centered, group = BB.text$year))+
  > geom_boxplot(aes(fill = BB.sentiment$year),
  outlier.colour = "black", outlier.shape = 16, outlier.size = 2)
```

```
# add labels to our boxplot using xlab ("Year"),
ylab("Sentiment(Centered)"), and ggtitle          # ("Economic
Sentiment - Beige Book (2011-2013)")
> BB.boxplot<- BB.boxplot + xlab("Year") + ylab("Sentiment
(Centered)") +
   ggtitle("Economic Sentiment - Beige Book (2011-2013)")
# draw boxplot
BB.boxplot
```

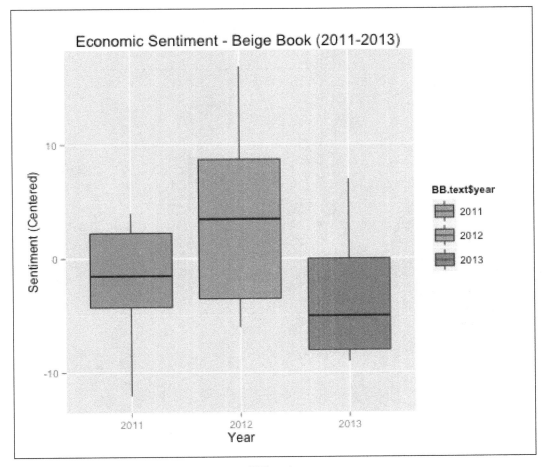

BB.boxplot

This simple example exposes some interesting insight into the economic conditions in the United States as reflected by the *Beige Book*. The x axis shows year and the y axis reflects mean-centered sentiment. Immediately, we can see that both 2011 and 2013 were below the mean sentiment over the entire document space (with the mean of 2013 below that of 2011). The boxplot shows us that while 2012 was above the mean, it had quite a bit of variability as reflected by the large interquartile range. We can also use this visualization to make comparisons between years—note that 2011 has a higher median value than 2013 but also has lower values as shown by the lower hinge. We can also reduce the data to month-by-year instead of merely year to potentially expose further patterns and increased variability. The following boxplot uses a larger portion of the data and reflects the ups and downs of sentiment over time:

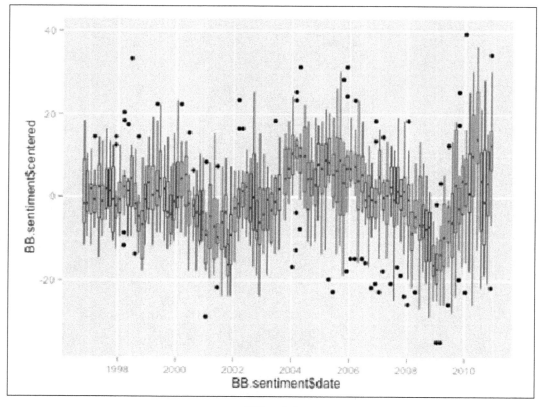

BB.boxplot

The screenshot after the following example shows economic sentiment with recession bars highlighted (2001-2002, 2007-2009):

```
# this code can be used to add the recession bars shown below where
xmin and xmax    # are used to add vertical columns to our plot.
```

```
> rect2001 <- data.frame (
  xmin=2001, xmax=2002, ymin=-Inf, ymax=Inf)
> rect2007 <- data.frame (
  xmin=2007, xmax=2009, ymin=-Inf, ymax=Inf)


# ggplot is an R package used for advanced plotting.
> BB.boxplot <- ggplot(BB.sentiment, aes(x=BB.sentiment$year, y=BB.
sentiment$centered,    group=BB.sentiment$year))
> BB.boxplot <- BB.boxplot + geom_boxplot(outlier.colour = "black",
    outlier.shape = 16, outlier.size = 2)
> BB.boxplot <- BB.boxplot + geom_rect(data=rect2001, aes(xmin=xmin,
    xmax=xmax, ymin=-Inf, ymax=+Inf), fill='pink', alpha=0.2,
inherit.aes = FALSE)
> BB.boxplot <- BB.boxplot + geom_rect(data=rect2007, aes(xmin=xmin,
    xmax=xmax, ymin=-Inf, ymax=+Inf), fill='pink', alpha=0.2,
inherit.aes = FALSE)
> BB.boxplot <- BB.boxplot + xlab("Date") + ylab("Sentiment
    (Centered)") + ggtitle("Economic Sentiment - Beige Book (1996-
2010)")
> BB.boxplot
```

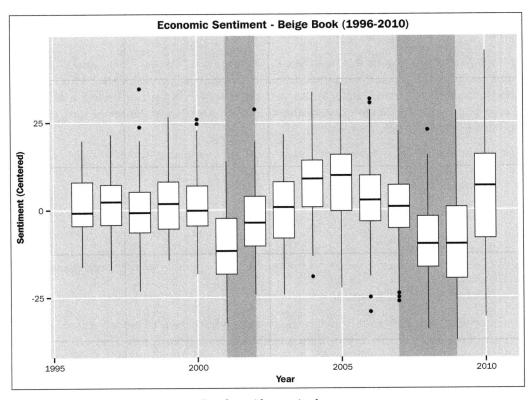

Boxplots with recession bars

Case study 2 – Naive Bayes classifier

In the previous chapter, we described how Naive Bayes is a type of classifier, that is, a statistical model designed to estimate group membership of observations. If we have a sufficient amount of training data, we can use it to train or learn a statistical model that we can subsequently use to estimate the sentiment of other, unlabeled observations. The key assumption underlying this technique is that at least some words are used with different frequencies by those with positive and negative sentiments towards a particular target. This section walks through the implementation of Naive Bayes for sentiment classification.

For demonstrative purposes, we have scraped about 4,000 tweets using the methods set out in *Chapter 3, Mining Twitter with R*. About half include the hashtag #prolife, and the other half include the hashtag #prochoice. It seems likely that these tweets satisfy the earlier assumption; that is, tweets using each of these opposing hashtags likely use different words and phrases to a different extent. The following code sets up a data frame of the tweets and appends the variable "hash" (as in hashtag) to the data frame, where 1 denotes the use of #prochoice and 0 denotes the use of #prolife. As this is a supervised method, we use the hashtags as labels for the supervised learning process. The results of the model will allow us to categorize unlabeled tweets in future.

Suppose that all the tweets are in a list called abortion_tweets, as would be output by the searchTwitter function introduced in *Chapter 3, Mining Twitter with R*. Also, suppose that we've created a vector named hash, which is a set of 1's repeating for the number of prochoice tweets concatenated with a vector of zeroes as long as the number of prolife tweets, as follows:

```
# generate a data frame from the list of tweets
> require(twitteR)
> twtsdf<- twListToDF(abortion_tweets)

> twtsdf$hash<- hash

# Drop unneeded variables from the data frame
> keeps <- c("text", "id", "retweetCount", "isRetweet", "screenName", "hash")
> twtsdf<- twtsdf[,keeps]
```

The following loop generates a list of the tweets, where each tweet is broken into a vector of separate words rather than a sentence. It also compiles a list of the usernames, called names. Lastly, we separate and keep the vector of hashtags and name it outcome as shown in the following code snippet:

```
> list.vector.words<- list()
> allwords<- NULL

> names<- NULL
  for (i in 1:dim(twtsdf)[1]){
    each.vector<- strsplit(twtsdf$text[i], split="")
    names<- c(names, twtsdf$screenName[i])
    allwords<- c(allwords, each.vector)
    list.vector.words[[i]] <- each.vector
}


> outcome<- twtsdf$hash
```

Next, we use the `tm` package to create a corpus like the one shown in *Chapter 3, Mining Twitter with R*. Also, we'll remove the hashtags, as we are going to treat that information as labels for the supervised learning process as follows:

```
>require(tm)
# make a corpus
> dat.tm <- Corpus(VectorSource(list.vector.words))
# convert all words to lowercase
> dat.tm <- tm_map(dat.tm, tolower)
# remove punctuation
> dat.tm <- tm_map(dat.tm, removePunctuation)
# remove the hashtags
> dat.tm <- tm_map(dat.tm, removeWords, words=c("prochoice"))
> dat.tm <- tm_map(dat.tm, removeWords, words=c("prolife"))
# remove extra white space
> dat.tm <- tm_map(dat.tm, stripWhitespace)
# stem all words
> dat.tm <- tm_map(dat.tm, stemDocument)
```

Next, we create a document-term matrix, with one twist. Instead of using single words, we use bigrams (ordered two-word pairs). Thus, instead of breaking the sentence "See spot run" into three single words, we make two bigrams, "see spot" and "spot run." This helps us capture more nuance than single words, which helps deal with extreme sentiments and negation as follows:

```
# create a bigram tokenizer using the RWeka package
> require(RWeka)
> BigramTokenizer<- function(x) NGramTokenizer(x, Weka_control(min =
2, max = 2))
# create the document-term matrix
> datmat<- DocumentTermMatrix(dat.tm, control = list(tokenize =
BigramTokenizer))
> dat<- as.matrix(datmat)
# Add user names as rownames to matrix
> rownames(dat) <- names
```

Only bigrams that are used by a sufficient number of authors are useful. Thus, we need a bit of code to remove bigrams that are uncommon. The following lines create a vector of the column sums (that is, the number of times each bigram is used) and then creates a table of those column sums:

```
> word.usage<- colSums(dat)
> table(word.usage)
```

There is no hard-and-fast rule about the lower limit on the number or proportion of uses of a bigram necessary to keep it. We recommend starting out with a low number, such as 9, and working upwards from there as shown in the following code:

```
# first, set all values in the matrix that are greater than 1 to 1
> dat[dat>1] <- 1
> threshold <- 9  # set a threshold
> tokeep <- which(word.usage>threshold)
# find which column sums are above the threshold
# keep all rows, and only columns with sums greater than the threshold
> dat.out<- dat[,tokeep]
```

The last processing step is to drop users who use a very small number of bigrams. The logic is the same as when we dropped the least common bigrams: users who use different words from all the other users are hard to model. Again, there is a bit of art here. We recommend only keeping users who used at least two bigrams, though you may want to increase this if the documents you are using are larger than tweets, as shown in the following code:

```
# Drop users with few words....
# find how many zeroes are in each row
> num.zero <- rowSums(dat.out==0)

# explore data by making a table; can inform choice of cutoff
> table(num.zero)
# the number of columns of the document bigram matrix
> num_cols <- dim(dat.out)[2]
# users must have used this many bigrams to scale
> cutoff <- 2
# create a list of authors to keep
> authors_tokeep <- which(num.zero <(num_cols-cutoff))
# keep only users with 2 bigrams
> dat.drop <- dat.out[authors_tokeep,]
# similarly, drop those users from the vector of hashtags
> outcome <- outcome[authors_tokeep]
```

Finally, we are ready to implement the model. To do so, we'll load the `e1071` package, a general-purpose data-mining package. Then, we set up the data so that it is back in the data frame format, with the `outcome` variable, `hash`, turned into a factor. Factors are data storage types that are good for holding integer-valued variables, as shown in the following code:

```
> require(e1071)
# append the outcome to the first column of dat.drop
> myDat <- cbind(outcome, dat.drop)
# turn the doc-term matrix into a data frame
> myDat <- as.data.frame(myDat)
# turn the outcome variable (first column) into a factor
> myDat[,1] <- as.factor(myDat[,1])
```

Finally, a single line of code implements the model. We will save the model as an object called `NBmod`. The first argument to the `NaiveBayes` function lists the predictors, while the second argument gives the `outcome` variable. We use a trick to capture all of the columns of `myDat` except the first one; using a negative number means "include all but this item", as shown in the following code:

```
# run the model; save the results to an object
> NBmod<- naiveBayes(myDat[,-1], myDat[,1])
```

We should expect our model to perform well on the data on which it was trained, or "in sample". To get a sense of how our model performed, we can make a confusion matrix that compares actual values of the `outcome` variable to predicted values as follows:

```
# generate a vector of predictions
# arguments: estimated model, predictors, outcome to predict
> NBpredictions <- predict(NBmod, myDat[,-1])
# pull out the actual outcomes
> actual<- myDat[,1]
# make the confusion matrix
> table(NBpredictions, actual, dnn=list("predicted", "actual"))

          actual
predicted      0        1
        0     339       24
        1     617      825
```

Elements in this table on the main diagonal (the top-left and bottom-right cells) are correctly predicted. The table shows that, in the sample, our **percent correctly predicted (PCP)** is about 65 percent. The degree to which our model is accurate will be a function of several parameters. First, the more training data we use, the more accurate our model will be (in sample). Second, the model's accuracy will increase with the divergence in the word-use patterns between our two sentiment groups. Lastly, the larger the documents included in this type of analysis, the better the accuracy of the model. Thus, this model is a bit tenuous for Twitter data and only achieves a modest in-sample accuracy.

The point of this type of model is not to check its accuracy on existing sentiment data. Rather, we want to use this model to predict the sentiment of unlabeled observations. One simple way to accomplish this is to preprocess the unlabeled data along with the labeled data. Then, estimate the model on only the labeled data. Finally, use the trained model to predict the values of the unlabeled observations. To simulate this, suppose we had preprocessed some data as we did earlier but with 500 #prolife and 500 #prochoice tweets and additionally 100 tweets with the hashtag #abortion. Then, we could estimate the model and predict the values of the 100 unlabeled tweets with the following code:

```
# run the model on the 1000 labelled instances
> NBmod<- naiveBayes(myDat[1:1000,-1], myDat[1:1000,1])
# predict outcomes for the last 100 unlabeled instances
> NBpredictions<- predict(NBmod, myDat[1001:1100,-1])
# make a table of the predictions
> table(NBpredictions)

actual
predicted       0          1
        0          24         0
        1          27        49
```

Interestingly, this model predicts better on the test set than on the training set (73 percent accuracy). This is a bit of an anomaly; generally, we should not expect test results to be stronger than training accuracies, unless, by some chance, the test data is more well behaved than the training data. Overall, the Naive Bayes classifier is a useful tool for estimating sentiment valence. It is quick to estimate and has reasonable accuracy. However, as we saw in this example, it requires training data with binary scores already assigned.

Case study 3 – IRT models for unsupervised sentiment scaling

The theoretical underpinnings of IRT models were set out in the previous chapter. Here, we briefly review them before demonstrating how to implement this class of models. However, readers should note that this class of model is cutting-edge, to the point of being considered experimental.

IRT models for text analysis start with the strong assumption that texts (or authors thereof) lie along a continuum, and that this continuum directly affects their word choices in a monotonic way such that if word use is likely at one end of the spectrum, it is unlikely at the other. These assumptions are somewhat restrictive; we can only scale texts that deal with moderately narrow topics and that are subject to word choice differences. Furthermore, it is important that the sentiment continuum be that underlying continuum; else, the model will estimate whatever continuum underlies the data. A good example would be the debate about the Affordable Care Act, wherein liberals occasionally refer to it by name, while conservatives are more likely to refer to it as Obamacare. Note that for IRT methods to function, these differences only have to be probabilistic (that is, some liberals certainly call it Obamacare some of the time), and these word choice differences have to be consistent across a number of terms, not just one.

As an example, we can use the same Twitter data set out in the section on Naive Bayes. We should suspect that these tweets meet the assumptions made earlier, namely, there is a single underlying continuum of sentiment about a single moderately narrow topic, and that that continuum likely affects the word choice of each author.

The preprocessing steps are very similar to those of the Naive Bayes application discussed in the previous section. To begin, take the same initial steps: collect tweets with one (or more) searchTwitter call(s); turn them into a data frame called tweetsdf; and append an outcome variable called hash to this data frame. Again, these steps are exactly the same as the ones discussed earlier, and are thus not repeated. One difference is that, before continuing, we will drop retweets from the data frame. The reason is that including a large number of retweets affects scaling negatively. It is a best practice to drop the retweets and then just give all tweets with the same text the same scale after running the IRT model. The following line of code in English reads: put into twtsdf all of the rows in twtsdf where the variable isRetweet is FALSE.

```
> twtsdf<- twtsdf[twtsdf$isRetweet == FALSE,]
```

Next, we continue following the Naive Bayes preprocessing steps by dropping the unnecessary variables from the data frame. After that, we execute the `for` loop that generates our list of vectors of words, create a corpus, and turn it into a document-term matrix, just as done earlier. We normalize all cells to one, and then drop infrequent bigrams, as in the Naïve Bayes example.

The second difference in the preprocessing steps for IRT is that we need to aggregate all of the tweets by user, that is, collapse the document-term matrix such that there is only one row per user instead of one row per tweet. This step follows from the fact that IRT models assume that all of an author's word choices are affected by his or her position on the underlying continuum. Thus, we aggregate all of their tweets together as shown in the following code snippet:

```
# pull out list of words
> words<- colnames(dat.out)
# aggregate by rowname (i.e. twitter user name), and sum rows with the
same user name
> dat.agg<- aggregate(dat.out, list(rownames(dat.out)), sum)
# aggregating makes a variable called Group.1; turn this back into the
matrix rowname
> names<- dat.agg$Group.1
> dat.agg<- as.matrix(dat.agg[,2:dim(dat.agg)[2]])
# set cells greater than 1 back to 1
> dat.agg[dat.agg>1] <- 1
> rownames(dat.agg) <- names
```

This bit of code similarly aggregates our hashtag vector, which we will use for model checking later:

```
> outcomes<- as.matrix(twtsdf$hash)
> rownames(outcomes) <- rownames(dat.out)
> outcomes.agg <- aggregate(outcomes, list(rownames(outcomes)), mean)
> hashscores<- round(outcomes.agg$V1)
```

The final preprocessing step mimics that of Naive Bayes: we drop users who use a very small number of bigrams. In Twitter examples, we find that only keeping users who employ at least four key bigrams makes a good choice, though there is no hard-and-fast rule about this:

```
> num.zero <- rowSums(dat.agg==0)

# explore data by making a table; can inform choice of cutoff
> table(num.zero)
```

```
# the number of columns of the document bigram matrix
> num_cols <- dim(dat.out)[2]
# users must have used this many bigrams to scale
> cutoff <- 4
# create a list of authors to keep
> authors_tokeep <- which(num.zero <(num_cols-cutoff))
# keep only users with 2 bigrams
> dat.drop <- dat.out[authors_tokeep,]
# similarly, drop those users from the vector of hashtags
> outcome <- outcome[authors_tokeep]
```

After all that processing, we are ready to implement the model. The package we employ, `pscl`, was designed for political science uses, hence the mentions of legislators, votes, and roll-calls. The `rc` function sets up the data matrix for estimation, while the `ideal` function estimates the logistic model described in the previous chapter as follows:

```
> require(pscl)
> rc <- rollcall(data=dat.drop)       # sets up the data
# executes the model (this may take several minutes)
> jmod <- ideal(rc,store.item=T)
```

Now we have a new object named `jmod`. The `xbar` variable captures the scale positions of every author for whom we had enough data to scale. One thing we may want is a list of all of the scaled positions of all users as shown in the following code snippet:

```
> scaled.positions<- data.frame(jmod$xbar)       # make a new data frame
of the scale
> rownames(scaled.positions) <- rownames(dat.drop)
# make the rownames sensible
> colnames(scaled.positions) <- "scale"
# give the single variable a good name
> head(scaled.positions)
# list the first few scaled positions
# note: these are not real user names
scale
exUser1          0.739675498
exUser2         -0.099127391
exUser3          0.466915634
```

Another way to look at this data is to draw a histogram of all of the scaled positions:

```
> hist(jmod$xbar, main= "Scaled Positions of Twitter Users", xlab=
"relative position")
```

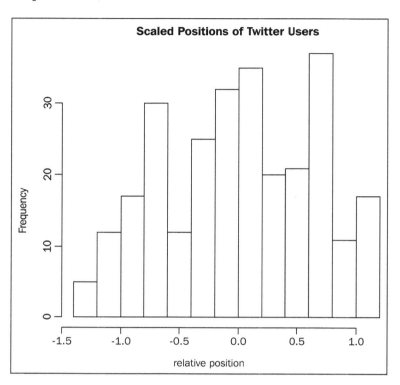

The histogram shows the overall distribution of positions in the data. Some care needs to be taken in interpreting these values. Foremost, these values are relative to one another. Put in a different way, these numbers describe distances between authors but not compared to any true values. This means that zero, rather than meaning neutral, probably means something closer to central. Similarly, the score only captures the fact that an author at zero is to the left of authors at 0.1, and to the right of authors at -0.1. This means that, had we *only* scaled the prochoice tweets, we still would have had a distribution centered at zero, even though all of the tweets being scaled would be to the right of center.

A second caution concerns authors scaled at or near zero. These may be centrist authors; however, authors
that are difficult to scale also end up in the center. This may be because they use few bigrams or because they use conflicting bigrams (some to the left and some to the right). The point is to note that zero may not mean center; it may also mean "I'm not sure".

Additionally, the model has no sense of left or right; it just assigns numbers to authors. To figure out whether authors with scores of +1 are liberals or conservatives, we need to examine the tweets of a couple of authors from each end. First, identify a handful of authors with large, positive scale values, and then go back to the original data frame and read their tweets. This should give you a sense of which end of the scale is which. Additionally, it should give you an idea of whether the underlying scale estimated corresponds to the latent dimension you had hoped to capture, that is, sentiment. The following is a list of positive authors:

```
> scaled.positions[scaled.positions$scale> 0.9,]
# generates a list of large, positive authors
# these are just examples, not real users
> MrTweeter          0.9137
> AnotherTweeter     0.9442
```

Then, go back to the original data frame and pull up the tweet(s) from those users. This should tell you if the people on the positive end of this scale are on the left or right. You should check several of these from both ends. People on the same end of the scale should have the same views, generally. If not, the model may have failed or pulled out an underlying continuum other than the one you were looking for!

```
> twtsdf[twtsdf$id== "MrTweeter",]
1    This would be MrTweeter's original tweet and hashtag.
```

Also, we may be interested in the `difficulty` and `discrimination` parameters of each bigram. We can get a sense of both by plotting one against the other. The `jmod$betabar[,2]` parameter is the difficulty parameter, and `jmod$betabar[,1]` is the discrimination parameter.

```
> plot(jmod$betabar[,2], jmod$betabar[,1],
    xlab="difficulty", ylab="discrimination", main="Bigrams")
```

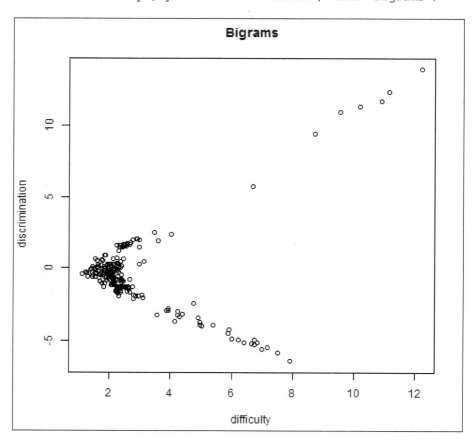

On this graph, each point represents a bigram. The x axis represents how hard it is for a user to use a bigram; essentially, this is a measure of the bigram's rarity. The y axis plots each bigram's discrimination, that is, the extent to which it is more likely to be used by those on one side of the scale or the other. For instance, bigrams with large, positive discrimination parameters are likely to be used by those on the right-hand side of the scale and unlikely to be used by those on the left-hand side. The sign determines left/right, and the magnitude represents how strong the effect is. Bigrams with near-zero discrimination parameters are equally used by authors on all parts of the scale. Examining this graph, we see that most bigrams are not discriminating between sides of the scale. Additionally, there is a strong correlation between difficulty and discrimination; bigrams that are used frequently do not discriminate much, whereas more infrequently used bigrams discriminate better. This is a classic pattern in scaling applications; absence of this type of *flying V* pattern is evidence that scaling has failed or that the model has picked up an underlying continuum that is bizarre or nonsensical.

If you want to get a sense of the most discriminating bigrams, you can generate a list with the following code, which uses the `plyr` package for its convenient `arrange()` function:

```
# identify which words have large discrimination parameters
# abs() returns the absolute value
> t <- which(abs(jmod$betabar[,1]) >1)
> twords<- colnames(dat.drop)[t]
> tnums<- jmod$betabar[,1][t]
# make a data frame of the discriminating words
> bigwords<- data.frame(twords, tnums)
> bigwords<- arrange(bigwords,desc(bigwords$tnums))
```

Finally, since we know what side of the abortion issue all of our users were on, we can plot them and color code the hashtag they used (this is why we saved the hashtags during data processing). In real, unsupervised sentiment analysis settings, you would not have this information, but since we do, we can use it to check the accuracy of the model as follows:

```
# make a vector, o, of the order of the scale positions
> o <- order(jmod$xbar)
# plot the scale against an arbitrary y value; zero to number of users
# color code each point according to its hashtag with the 'col'
parameter
> plot(jmod$xbar[o], seq(1:length(jmod$xbar)), col=-outcome[o]+3)
```

We've put the results of this code in the following graph, and also added a text callout of a couple of the tweets and a legend for readability. The code for the extras is simple and can be found on this book's web page on the Packt Publishing website:

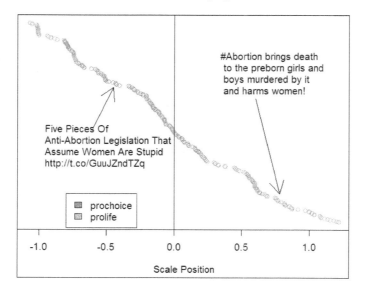

The x axis here represents the scale position, while the y axis is arbitrary. The green points are those tweets that used #prolife, whereas the red ones used #prochoice. We can see, generally, that most of the red points are to the left of zero, while most of the green points are to the right of zero. Thus, the model seems to have scaled most of these tweets accurately. However, the model has a tough time discriminating authors near the middle of the scale, which is common in scaling applications. Additionally, note the group of mis-characterized tweets in the upper-left corner. On further examination, these are users who tweeted prochoice-related phrases, but used them ironically. The model, not recognizing irony, incorrectly put these tweets with the prochoice tweets. This is a common hurdle in text analysis and represents a fruitful area for future research.

Summary

Social media mining is technical, and is occasionally as much an art as a science. We hope to have given readers a leg up on the subject by walking them through these extended case studies, each involving a different style of analysis. However, gaining a mastery of these techniques will certainly entail readers scraping their own text-based data, and applying the tools demonstrated here. As you do so, we hope you remain careful about the pitfalls listed in *Chapter 4, Potentials and Pitfalls of Social Media Data*, and proceed with due thought and care.

Conclusions and Next Steps

Social media has become ubiquitous, as has the understanding that harnessing it is crucial to measuring the sentiments of an increasingly plugged-in population. Ignoring this information while acknowledging its presence, whether for businesses or civic purpose, constitutes an informal logical fallacy. Those businesses, politicians, social movements, and researchers who choose to ignore this data do so at their own peril and to their own detriment.

Final thoughts

People are highly opinionated and compelled to share with others. The advent of the social web has given them a tremendous new venue to do so, and explains, in part, the explosive growth in text data. These personal opinions are valuable; rather than being fleeting or trivial, they are both predictive of and caused by individual intentions. Over the last decade, scholars and practitioners of social media mining have developed techniques to measure and thus glean insights from textual opinion data. These tools are crucial, especially since much text data does not come with easily quantifiable opinions such as the availability of stars, likes, or thumbs-ups that can be easily counted.

With the expanding availability of data and the increasing sophistication and usability of text data mining tools, social media mining is more accessible to a wide array of practitioners. An increasing number of social scientists, businesses, politicians, and media outlets put themselves at a stark disadvantage by ignoring this source of insight. Social scientists are now able to tap the sentiments of larger and harder-to-reach populations. Industries can now obtain granular reactions to products and adjust their offerings accordingly based on large samples, rather than a few poignant complaints. Politicians can gauge the desires of their constituents, the polarity of issues, and the effectiveness of their campaigns. Meanwhile, media outlets can not only track the interest in their stories, but also more easily take the pulse of the population on which they report.

The opinionated and plugged-in nature of people has driven the growth of text data; however, it is techniques like the ones outlined in this book that help add measurable value to that text. Techniques like the ones outlined in this book help explain the value of that text. Up until the last 40 years, these opinions were a part of small networks and shared mainly with first order neighbors. The data was hard if not impossible to collect, and few methods existed to examine the data. Nowadays, however, the data is available and the methods are maturing. We hope this book gives practitioners and scholars a quality entry point to the study and use of opinion mining techniques, and that it invests them with the knowledge necessary to explore textual data in a systematic and rigorous manner.

An expanding field

The field of sentiment analysis is growing quickly. Google Scholar reports nearly 70,000 articles including the words sentiment analysis published from 2012 to 2013; three and a half times as many as were published in the preceding annum. Assuredly, this growth is due in part to the wide array of purposes to which people apply sentiment analysis and text mining. Beyond the number of applications is the power of social media data; one study (Brynjolfsson, 2011) found that technology investments of 179 large publicly-traded firms that adopted data-driven decision making have output and productivity five to six percent higher than what would otherwise be expected; in an era when data provably matters for high-stakes decisions, being able to make new quantities measurable will certainly be a benefit. What would be the impact on your organization if you could improve output and productivity by a mere five to six percent? Or, what would be the social impact of a policy that was five to six percent more effective?

Before setting you off to conduct your own research, however, we again implore you to take care with your analyses, for they often come with consequences. Numbers, and especially measurements, tend to get reified in unhealthy ways such as IQ and BMI have been in the last two decades. Knowing this, it is especially important that you think hard about your measurements and deliver them with appropriate caveats. Consider carefully the population of people to which you can extrapolate; the users of social media are often young and urban. Furthermore, beware of contexts in which people have incentives to provide or promote biased opinions such as when writing about rivals. Lastly, carefully consider a new trend in paid opinion writing, wherein companies or advertisers hire tech-savvy authors to spam social media with favorable information about them. Detecting these strategic actors may in fact be an interesting research area in the field over the next decade. However, if you chose to analyze social data, the need will remain to be vigilant of its pitfalls. That said, the promise of social media data is great, if it can be leveraged with care.

Further reading

For more information, you can refer to the following books:

- *Taming Text: How to Find, Organize, and Manipulate It, Ingersoll, Morton,* and *Farris*: This is a pragmatic volume that covers exactly what its title promises. As data scientists, it has been noted that we spend around 80 percent of our time arranging our data for analysis. This book can help to trim that figure, allowing you to spend more time analyzing and interpreting, rather than data munging.

- *Mining the Social Web: Data Mining Facebook, Twitter, LinkedIn, Google+, GitHub, and More, Matthew Russell*: This is an excellent resource for practitioners wanting to learn how to get their hands on a wide array of social and web data. The book also features a companion piece that deals with analyzing social data. Readers should note that this pair of books utilizes Python rather than R.

- *Speech and Language Processing, Jurafski* and *Martin*: This book provides a slightly more advanced and fairly wide review of many techniques and technologies applied to language. This book is slightly more technical than *Social Media Mining in R*; it is likely inappropriate for those unfamiliar with optimization.

- *The Handbook of Computational Linguistics and Natural Language Processing, Clark, Fox,* and *Lappin*: This is another fairly broad book that covers many NLP topics, but with more of a focus on machine learning than theoretical statistics. It is suitable for graduate-level students and researchers.

- *Machine Learning with R, Brett Lanz*: This is a nice volume that covers a wide array of machine-learning algorithms. While not aimed specifically at social media, readers will find several of the techniques applicable.

- *Finding Groups in Data: An Introduction to Cluster Analysis, Kaufman* and *Rousseeuw*: This is a well-crafted book that makes an excellent first read on clustering techniques, which we mentioned in *Chapter 3, Mining Twitter with R*. The book covers several clustering techniques in an intuitive and non-technical manner.

- *A First Course in Statistical Programming with R, Braun* and *Murdoch*: This is an excellent resource for the world's most popular and fastest-growing statistical programming language. This book goes into great detail about programming constructs and graphical parameters, all with an eye towards building a student's competencies in applied statistics.

- *Designing Social Research, Normal Blaikie*: This is an excellent first book on research design. It carefully walks readers through knowledge areas such as theory testing, measurement, and inference.

Bibliography

- *Semisupervised Learning for Computational Linguistics, Steven Abney, Chapman and Hall,* 2007

- *Sentiment Analysis and Opinion Mining, Morgan & Claypool Publishers, Bing Liu,* May 2012

- *Designing Social Research (2nd Edition), Polity,* November 2009

- *A First Course in Statistical Programming with R, Braun.W. and Murdoch.D., Cambridge University Press,* 2007

- *Strength in Numbers: How Does Data-Driven Decision Making Affect Firm Performance?, Erik Brynjolfsson, ICIS 2011 Proceedings, Paper 13,* 2011

- *The Handbook of Computational Linguistics and Natural Language Processing, Clark.A., Fox.C., and Lappin.S., Wiley-Blackwell,* October 2012

- *The Statistical Analysis of Roll Call Data, Clinton.J., Jackman.S., and Rivers.D., American Political Science Review,* May 2004

- *Taming Text: How to Find, Organize, and Manipulate It, Ingersoll.G., Morton.T., and Farris.A., Manning Publications,* January 2013

- *Speech and Language Processing (2nd Edition), Jurafsky.D. and Martin.J., Pearson Prentice Hall,* May 2008

- *Finding Groups in Data: An Introduction to Cluster Analysis, Kaufman.L. and Rousseeuw.P., Wiley-Interscience,* March 2005

- *Machine Learning with R, Lantz and Brett, Packt Publishing,* October 2013

- *Mining the Social Web: Data Mining Facebook, Twitter, LinkedIn, Google+, GitHub, and More (2nd Edition), Matthew Russell, O'Reilly Media,* 2013

- *Consilience: The Unity of Knowledge, E. O. Wilson, Vintage,* March 1999

- About Me The Long Tail, n.p, n.d, Web, 10 Jan. 2014

- what's new on reddit: Reflections on the Recent Boston Crisis, blog.reddit, n.p, n.d, Web. 10 Jan. 2014

- *Fake Reviews: Amazon's Rotten Core, Forbes,* n.p, n.d, Web. 10 Jan. 2014

- *Gartner Blog Network,* n.p, n.d, Web, 10 Jan. 2014

- *Google Politics: Four Screens To Victory, Independent Voter Network IVN.us,* n.p, n.d, Web, 10 Jan. 2014

- *IBM big data platform Bringing big data to the Enterprise,* n.p, Web, 10 Jan. 2014

- *Key Facts-Facebook's latest news, announcements and media resources,* n.p, n.d, Web, 10 Jan. 2014

- *Open Innovation: Open Innovation Community*, n.p, n.d, Web, 10 Jan. 2014

- *Taboada et al. Lexicon-based Methods for Sentiment Analysis. Computational Linguistics*, Vol. 37, No 2, 2011

- *Twitter turns six*, Twitter blogs, n.p, n.d, Web, 10 Jan. 2014

- U.S. Distrust in Media Hits New High, Gallup.Com-Daily News, Polls, Public Opinion on Politics, Economy, Wellbeing, and World, n.p, n.d, Web, 10 Jan. 2014

- Welcome to the United Nations: It's Your World, n.p, n.d, Web, 10 Jan. 2014

- https://vimeo.com/11742135

- Social web, Wikipedia, the free encyclopedia, 16 Nov. 2013, Web, 10 Jan. 2014

- 50 Cent Party, Wikipedia, the free encyclopedia, 28 Nov. 2013, Web, 10 Jan. 2014

- You and Your Research Computer Science, U.Va. Engineering, graduate and undergraduate computer science programs, Master's degree, PhD, Virginia, n.p, n.d, Web, 10 Jan. 2014

Index

A

Amazon Web Services (AWS.tools) 22
Anscombe's quartet 29
application programming interface (API) 34
arguments 23
assignment operator 24

B

bccmpls 41
benefits, R 19
Big Data
  about 10, 11
  scope 12

C

carrot (>) operator 23
case studies, social media mining
  considerations 65, 66
  IRT models 91
  lexicon-based sentiment 67
  Naive Bayes classifier 86
corpus 38

D

data frames
  creating 26-28
data mining 8
dendrogram 41
Distributed Storage and List (dsl) 22
dist variable 28
document-term matrix
  building 39
Dropbox 42

F

Facebook 9
FAQs, R 20
files
  importing 26-28
function 23

G

Git 42
GitHub 42
GNU (GNU's Not Unix) 20
Google Drive 42
Google Reviews 57
graphical user interface (GUI) 22

H

HadoopInteractiVE (hive) 22
Hadoop Steaming (HadoopSteaming) 22
help function 24
hierarchical agglomerative clustering 40
honest signals 12-14
human sensors 12-14

I

information bounce 10
installation, R 22
integrated development environment
      (IDE) 22
Internet Movie Database (IMDB) 59
IRT models 63
IRT models case study 91-98
Item Response Theory (IRT) 62, 63

L

lexicon-based case study 67-84
lexicon-based sentiment classification 59-61
lisarosie 41
logical operators 24

M

modifiable areal unit problem (MAUP) 49

N

Naive Bayes classifier 61, 62
Naive Bayes classifier case study 86-90
natural language processing (NLP) 7
nontraditional social data
   versus, traditional social data 46, 47

O

OAuthFactory function 35
operators, R
   arithmetic 23
   assignment 24
   logical 24
opinion mining. *See* also sentiment
     analysis 43
ordinary least squares (OLS) 27

P

plot() function 29
preliminary analyses 38-41
ProjectTemplate
   URL 42

Q

qualitative approaches
   using 16

R

R
   additional resources 30
   benefits 19
   community 21
   consequences 21
   FAQs 20
   installing 22
   URL, for FAQs 22
R code
   URL, for info 30
   writing, tips 30
references 101
registerTwitterOAuth function 35
RStudio
   about 20, 22
   URL 22

S

Scherers typology of emotions
   about 56
   attitudes 56
   emotion 56
   interpersonal stance 56
   mood 56
   personality traits 56
sentiment 56
sentiment analysis 100 7
sentiment polarity
   measuring 57, 59
seq() function 25
sequences
   about 25
   example 25
social media
   sentiments, measuring 44, 45
social media data
   inferential challenges 47-50
   measurements 47-49
   overview 46

pitfalls 43, 44
potentials 43
social media mining 99
about 7, 53
case studies 65
concepts 53, 54
content, identifying 57
content, retrieving 57
lexicon-based sentiment 59
Naive Bayes classifiers 61
URL, for code 8
with sentiment analysis 7, 8
Stack Overflow 21
state of communication section 8-10
stop words 38

T

**Text Mining Distributed Corpus Plug-In
(tm.plug.dc) 22**
traditional social data
versus, nontraditional social data 46, 47
traditional social science data
versus, social media data 54, 55
tweets 38, 57

Twitter
about 10, 33
URL, for developer account 34
Twitter data 57
about 43
need for 33
obtaining 34-37
twitteR package 34
Twittersphere 57

V

vectors
about 25
example 25
visualization 28, 29

W

weak ties 33
WordCloud package 38
World Wide Web (WWW) 9

Y

Yelp 57

Thank you for buying
Social Media Mining with R

About Packt Publishing

Packt, pronounced 'packed', published its first book "*Mastering phpMyAdmin for Effective MySQL Management*" in April 2004 and subsequently continued to specialize in publishing highly focused books on specific technologies and solutions.

Our books and publications share the experiences of your fellow IT professionals in adapting and customizing today's systems, applications, and frameworks. Our solution based books give you the knowledge and power to customize the software and technologies you're using to get the job done. Packt books are more specific and less general than the IT books you have seen in the past. Our unique business model allows us to bring you more focused information, giving you more of what you need to know, and less of what you don't.

Packt is a modern, yet unique publishing company, which focuses on producing quality, cutting-edge books for communities of developers, administrators, and newbies alike. For more information, please visit our website: www.packtpub.com.

About Packt Open Source

In 2010, Packt launched two new brands, Packt Open Source and Packt Enterprise, in order to continue its focus on specialization. This book is part of the Packt Open Source brand, home to books published on software built around Open Source licenses, and offering information to anybody from advanced developers to budding web designers. The Open Source brand also runs Packt's Open Source Royalty Scheme, by which Packt gives a royalty to each Open Source project about whose software a book is sold.

Writing for Packt

We welcome all inquiries from people who are interested in authoring. Book proposals should be sent to author@packtpub.com. If your book idea is still at an early stage and you would like to discuss it first before writing a formal book proposal, contact us; one of our commissioning editors will get in touch with you.

We're not just looking for published authors; if you have strong technical skills but no writing experience, our experienced editors can help you develop a writing career, or simply get some additional reward for your expertise.

Data Manipulation with R

ISBN: 978-1-78328-109-1   Paperback: 102 pages

Perform group-wise data manipulation and deal with large datasets using R efficiently and effectively

1. Perform factor manipulation and string processing.

2. Learn group-wise data manipulation using plyr.

3. Handle large datasets, interact with database software, and manipulate data using sqldf.

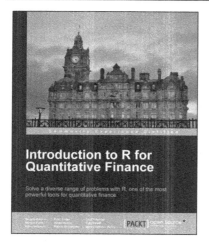

Introduction to R for Quantitative Finance

ISBN: 978-1-78328-093-3   Paperback: 164 pages

Solve a diverse range of problems with R, one of the most powerful tools for quantitative finance

1. Use time series analysis to model and forecast house prices.

2. Estimate the term structure of interest rates using prices of government bonds.

3. Detect systemically important financial institutions by employing financial network analysis.

Please check **www.PacktPub.com** for information on our titles

R Statistical Application Development by Example Beginner's Guide

ISBN: 978-1-84951-944-1   Paperback: 344 pages

Learn R Statistical Application Development from scratch in a clear and pedagogical manner

1. A self-learning guide for the user who needs statistical tools for understanding uncertainty in computer science data.

2. Essential descriptive statistics, effective data visualization, and efficient model building.

3. Every method explained through real data sets enables clarity and confidence for unforeseen scenarios.

Instant R Starter

ISBN: 978-1-78216-350-3   Paperback: 54 pages

Jump into the R programming language and go beyond "Hello World"

1. Learn something new in an Instant! A short, fast, focused guide delivering immediate results.

2. Basic concepts of the R language.

3. Discover tips and tricks for working with R.

4. Learn manipulation of R objects to easily customize your code.

Please check **www.PacktPub.com** for information on our titles